C. Lyons .

HOW TO INFLUENCE CHILDREN

HOW TO INFLUENCE CHILDREN

A Handbook of
Practical Parenting Skills

Charles Schaefer, Ph. D.

The Children's Village
Dobbs Ferry, N.Y.

VNR **VAN NOSTRAND REINHOLD COMPANY**

NEW YORK   CINCINNATI   ATLANTA   DALLAS   SAN FRANCISCO
LONDON   TORONTO   MELBOURNE

Van Nostrand Reinhold Company Regional Offices:
New York Cincinnati Atlanta Dallas San Francisco

Van Nostrand Reinhold Company International Offices:
London Toronto Melbourne

Copyright © 1978 by Litton Educational Publishing, Inc.

Library of Congress Catalog Card Number: 77-20833
ISBN: 0-442-27370-3 cloth
       0-442-27371-1 paper

Manufactured in the United States of America

Published by Van Nostrand Reinhold Company
135 West 50th Street, New York, N.Y. 10020

Published simultaneously in Canada by Van Nostrand Reinhold Ltd.

15 14 13 12 11 10 9 8 7 6 5 4 3 2

Library of Congress Cataloging in Publication Data

Schaefer, Charles.
    How to influence children.

    Includes index.
    1. Children—Management. I. Title.
HQ769.S277   649'.1   77-20833
ISBN 0-442-27370-3
ISBN 0-442-27371-1 pbk.

To My Family

Mom and Dad,
My wife Anne,
Children Eric and Karine
and a special family friend, Lucy

Other books by Charles Schaefer

THERAPIES FOR CHILDREN—A HANDBOOK OF
EFFECTIVE TREATMENTS FOR PROBLEM BEHAVIORS
(with H. Millman)   1977

THERAPEUTIC USE OF CHILD'S PLAY   1976

DEVELOPING CREATIVITY IN CHILDREN   1973

BECOMING SOMEBODY—CREATIVE ACTIVITIES FOR
PRESCHOOL CHILDREN   1973

YOUNG VOICES—THE POETRY OF CHILDREN   1970

PREFACE

Research has shown that the stresses involved in becoming a parent are more severe than those involved in adjusting to marriage or to an occupation. Although raising children is one of the most joyful, enchanting, and rewarding occupations, it is also an exhausting and confusing job with built-in hardships and conflicting needs. It has been aptly described as a combination of "tough times, and tender moments." Middle class parents, in particular, seem to feel the stresses of parenting quite acutely. The purpose of this book is to help relieve these stresses by offering the reader a number of practical, concrete ideas for raising children. The ideas are based upon an extensive review of the literature on childrearing, common sense, and my own experience as a parent and child psychologist. Although most of the ideas presented are not new or original, they represent important aspects of childrearing that can be easily overlooked, forgotten, or taken for granted. This book, then, is designed to be a consciousness raising experience for those interested in the topic of effective parenting or child-raising.

Parenting is a very complex process, with many facets to it. Notwithstanding the low status and low remuneration our society has assigned to childrearing, it is an endeavor that is stimulating intellectually. The more you know about specific practices and understand how to use them the smoother and more efficient your childrearing will be. I have attempted to break down the complex process of parenting into a number of specific skills and attitudes that can be studied, remembered, and practiced in an efficient way. Although a number of the ideas in this book are not completely independent of one another, they all seem to have a different emphasis or approach to warrant consideration in their own right. This is a practical book, then, that focuses on specific skills of parenting rather than on broad, theoretical approaches.

This handbook provides a broad overview of childrearing practices. The definitions and descriptions of each skill are meant to offer a frame of reference or structure for organizing and clarifying the reader's thoughts. The succinct "how to" format is designed to provide a blueprint for action, and allow for quick and easy retrieval of information.

I have found most books on parenting to be rather wordy, anecdotal, or full of jargon. As a result, I have tried to keep this book clear, concise, and succinct. I do this at the risk of oversimplification, but I am confident that parents will be stimulated to study, discuss, and evaluate the ideas in greater depth. This is really an open-ended book, to be completed by parents in terms of their personal reactions, associations, and experiences. To further develop their understanding and expertise, parents should take advantage of education and discussion groups, courses on childrearing, and in-depth readings.

The comprehensive scope of this book may be somewhat overwhelming to some readers, but it is based on the fact that there are many ways to influence children. Like the master woodcarver who has over 300 special tools at his fingertips, the master parent is knowledgeable of and proficient in a wide variety of social influencing techniques. Some methods, of course, will be more useful than others, but all should be helpful on specific occasions. Since it is felt that you will be more effective if you bring to bear the full range of available influencing techniques — indeed it is almost inevitable that you will use most of them — the goal of this book is to make you more aware and effective in your use of many different methods.

Eclectic in design, this book presents practices based on diverse theoretical approaches to understanding children. Parenting methods are still in a state of healthy infancy, relying on a mixture of intuitive artistry and scientific methodology. An open "technical eclecticism" rather than a closed allegiance to one theoretical position is much needed with respect to techniques. Freudian, problem-solving, communication-focused, behavior modification, relationship-oriented, and humanistic approaches all have something to offer parents in regard to understanding and helping children. Thus the reader will find techniques based on the above theories as well as other rationales.

The focus of both parts of this book is on *positive,* i.e., self-enhancing for the child, influencing procedures rather than punitive self-deprecatory ones. Another criterion for the selection of skills for this book was practicality. I attempted to locate skills that had proven effective in actual practice, as opposed to the influencing techniques that seemed founded more in theory or speculation. For each skill the reader should find enough details and examples to begin incorporating the skill into his daily interactions with children. The orientation of this book, then, can best be described as eclectic, utilitarian, and empirical. Hopefully, future research will both deepen our understanding of the parenting skills presented herein, i.e., when, how, and with what type of child can each skill be best employed, and broaden the number of useful parenting skills available to us.

Rather than infallible pronouncements, the techniques described in this book should be viewed as tentative guidelines for action which, in my opinion, are based on the best available knowledge and theory. It should be noted that there is still much disagreement among the "experts" on childrearing. Some feel you should never spank a child, others feel spanking is not only permissible but necessary for effective parenting. Since there is no one right way to raise children, parents must decide for themselves which philosophies and methods seem most reasonable and applicable to them. Hopefully you will read the recommended procedures in this book with an open but critical mind. Your criteria for using any of the suggested techniques should be: does it make sense, and will it work for me?

In my opinion, the existing limitations in our knowledge and skills make it imperative that parents be committed to being experimental and tentative in the use of parenting practices. Parents should be ready to be guided by the research data on childrearing as well as the personal experiences of other parents, and be always ready to try other procedures. The hallmark of a science is to seek new knowledge by systematic observation, study, and experimentation. Parenting today is in the beginning stages of becoming a science and profession. Until recently it could have been described as intuitive and important, but rather indescribable and unquantifiable. Some people did it well, some poorly, and it was difficult to tell anyone how to do it. Many thought it would just naturally fall into place if you just gave tender loving care. It is now recognized that there is a great deal of scientific information about human behavior which can be applied with profit by parents. By taking courses on "How to Communicate with Children" and "How to be an Effective Parent," parents are discovering that alternate methods of relating to children really work. Parenting, like any other complex behavior, such as tennis or golf, can be broken down into specific components which can be clearly understood and practiced until one becomes natural and proficient at them. Hopefully, more and more parents will become committed to lifelong learning and experimentation in order to optimize their effectiveness with children. Rather than blind, intuitive, or natural parenting, wherein there is no body of knowledge passed along to succeeding generations or accountability for what you are doing, it seems more sensible to make parenting and child care more of a science and profession, and bring it out of the "dark ages."

This compendium of parenting practices is divided into two major parts. The first part of the book concerns ways of establishing effective discipline. The discipline part of the book is further subdivided into two sections, "Child Management Skills" and "Child Guidance Skills." The management skills refer to ways parents can manage or control children's behavior. The child guidance skills describe ways for parents to teach and help children to develop internal controls and self-coping skills. The second part of the book relates to the formation of close parent-child attachments and describes ways parents can foster positive family relationships.

An added feature of this book is the Appendix which reviews some basic principles of child development. Essentially, the main goal of parenting is child growth and development. Achieving this means that parents must be tuned in to the behavioral aspects of growth and development. Since parents are assigned the prime responsibility of socializing a child, the focus of this Appendix is on the development of the personality, sociality, and morality of children.

This book is written primarily for parents and students who wish to improve their ability to influence children. It should also be of interest to professionals who work with children or whose role it is to advise parents as to effective childrearing practices. This book can be used as a text or supplementary reading for parent education groups, and courses on childrearing, parenting, child management, or social influence.

CHARLES SCHAEFER, PHD.

CONTENTS

Section B.   Child Guidance Skills

Part II.   Ways to Build Positive Family Relationships / 131

HOW
TO
INFLUENCE
CHILDREN

Part I
Ways to Establish
Effective Discipline

INTRODUCTION

For the very true beginning of wisdom is the desire of discipline;
And the care of discipline is love.

Apocrypha

Discipline, in this book, is used in the broad sense to mean any teaching, guidance, or encouragement by adults which is designed to help children learn to live as socialized beings and achieve their optimum growth and development. The essence of discipline is to teach and it is derived from the biblical word disciple or one who follows the teachings of a leader. The immediate goal of discipline is to make your children disciples by teaching them both appropriate and inappropriate forms of behavior. The long term goal of discipline is the development of *self-control* and *self-direction,* i.e., children who can direct themselves without external control. Internal control means governing one's own behavior by using explicit norms, standards, and rules that have been internalized. Parents, then, should be continually seeking to work themselves out of the job of disciplinarian by gradually developing this skill in children.

There is probably no other aspect of childrearing that creates more interest or concern in parents than discipline. In the first part of the book, we will discuss ways of becoming more effective disciplinarians or teachers. Imparting discipline is a teaching process for you and a learning process for the child. There have been thousands of scientific research studies to guide us how to best teach children so as to maximize learning. Although there are many effective teaching methods available, most parents have become skilled in only a few. The most effective type of discipline involves the use of positive approaches (e.g., setting an example, persuasion, praise) much more than negative methods (e.g., punishment).

A positive approach is one in which your intention is to teach a child more adaptive ways of behaving while you show respect, acceptance, and support. With a positive approach, you view and treat a child as a friend rather than an adversary. As a result, the child feels that you are with him rather than against him. A negative or punitive influence approach, on the other hand, has as one of its goals hurting a child by inflicting physical or psychological pain e.g., loss of self-esteem, intense fearfulness, anxiety, or guilt. Punitive techniques devalue a child and belittle his importance as a human being. Examples of punitive techniques are insults, sarcasm, ridicule, threats, shouting at or beating a child, and disapproval of the whole child ("You're a bad child!"). While these negative methods are often effective in temporarily stopping misbehavior, their adverse effect on the psychological well-being of the child make them inappropriate for effective parenting.

To be effective, discipline should meet three criteria: 1) to produce a desired change or growth in the child; 2) maintain the child's self-esteem; and 3) keep a close relationship between parent and child. As mentioned before, the use of frequent and/or severe punishment runs a high risk of both lowering a child's sense of worth and causing the child to feel fearful and/or resentful towards the adult. On the other hand, the use of punishment or penalties has its place in childrearing and its proper application will be described in the Chapter on "Imposing Penalties."

It should be clear from reading the first part of this book that while discipline and punishment are interrelated they are far from being synonymous. Punishment is just one aspect of the multi-faceted disciplinary approach advocated in this book.

The first part on effective discipline is subdivided into "Child Management" and "Child Guidance." The management section refers to specific practices for directly influencing a child to do something the parent desires, or to stop performing an inappropriate act. The guidance section presents methods for teaching children to cope with the outside world while developing their abilities and discovering their true identity. The management section, then, describes ways of directly applying external controls on children, while the guidance section contains more indirect methods of promoting self-control and self-development in children.

Section A
Child Management Skills

PERMITTING

Behavior

Children are naturally noisy, impulsive, demanding and unpredictable. They challenge an adult's expectations of order, cleanliness, and propriety.

Some of the behavior of children, while unpleasant for parents, must be tolerated with good grace and without reproach. Permitting means accepting the harmless childishness of children and not expecting them to be miniature adults.

Among the behaviors that you must expect and permit are:

Stepping and playing in mud puddles.

Yelling and shouting during physically active games.

Messy floors while children are playing.

Continual physical activity by school age children.

Dirty clothes after playing.

Carelessness, forgetfulness, and tactlessness.

Tolerating certain of these behaviors with composure in no way implies that you approve of them or expect them to continue over the long run, e.g., carelessness or thanklessness. Nor is it a license for children to do whatever they wish with no regard for the rights of others.

Feelings

Every child is at times quite angry with his parents. If you allow your child to freely express and ventilate these hostile feelings, they will normally dissipate very quickly. If, on the other hand, the angry, resentful feelings towards parents are not allowed expression in the home, then the chances are they will build up inside the child and seek release in such forms as: hostile fantasies of injuring or killing parents; passive-aggressive actions such as pouting, apathy-withdrawal, not talking or cooperating; and scapegoating-bullying others.

Acknowledging the right of a child to express negative feelings to you (including anxious-fearful feelings) does not mean that you condone or approve of these feelings. It merely indicates that you expect these feelings to arise in the normal course of family living and that you believe that open communication fosters mutual understanding.

The extent of angry feelings or negative reactions tolerated will, of course, vary in accordance with the personal beliefs, values, and security of the parents. Some parents will only allow a child to identify his own feelings, e.g., "You made me very angry when you kept me in," or "Dad, I get very frightened of you when you spank me." Other parents put no limits on a child's verbal expressions, and do not become disturbed when a child curses at them or expresses a death wish, e.g., "I wish you were dead, I hate you!"

IGNORING

Some behavior of children is not normal childishness but immature behavior that the child is capable of controlling. Paradoxically, parents often reinforce this unwanted behavior by being critical of it. To criticize an act, you have to pay attention to the child, and, to some children, any form of parental attention − even unpleasant attention − is reinforcing.

Ignoring is a method of reducing inappropriate behavior in children (e.g., whining, quarreling, temper outbursts, crying) by deliberately paying no attention (in words and actions) to this behavior whenever it occurs. It means giving *absolutely no attention,* i.e., not looking at the child or acknowledging in any manner that the behavior is present. Initially the child will probably increase the misbehavior in an effort to force you to pay attention. If you persist, however, the child will soon get the message that you do not like and will not give any satisfaction to his unacceptable actions.

Guidelines

1. Only ignore behavior that can be safely tolerated, i.e., behavior that is not dangerous to the child or others.
2. Be sure you can indeed tolerate ignoring the behavior without eventually giving in or punishing the child. If a child is crying

or throwing a temper tantrum, you must be able to ignore this behavior 100 percent of the time and for however long it lasts. Assuming your previous attention had been reinforcing the act, if you remain firm you should begin to notice a gradual but steady decline in the duration and frequency of the misdeed. Eventually, it should die out completely.

3. If anyone else in the family is reinforcing the misdeed (sympathy from grandparents, smiling from siblings) you will have to convince them to ignore the behavior also.

4. If the misbehavior starts to really get to you, it may be necessary for you to go to another room to continue ignoring.

5. Remember to praise the child for behavior which is opposite of the undesired act, e.g., being pleasant rather than whiney.

6. Ignoring is a *slow* but *effective* method of eliminating problem behavior in children. It not only requires a lot of patience, but also will power since it is hard to ignore behavior that you don't like.

REDIRECTING

Redirection is a method of diverting and redirecting a child's energy to a substitute activity. It involves turning a child's attention from an objectionable pursuit to a neutral or more socially desirable one with the goal of inducing the child to lose interest in the original act. Diversions can be classified as either short term *distractions* or more long term *rechanneling* of unacceptable impulses or drives into constructive outlets.

Distractions

Often asking a simple question will suffice as a distraction. The question serves to interrupt the undesired act and simultaneously redirects the child's energy along more acceptable lines. If your child, for example, has the undesired habit of openly masturbating at home, you might try asking her in a calm and positive way about her day in school. If this is unsuccessful you might ask her to get you a glass of water. Your goal is to distract her from what she is doing without making her aware of what you are doing. Thus, you act as if you had a sudden thought − not that you are reproaching her. After repeated distracting incidents, your child may lose interest in the undesirable activity.

Also, when you see that children's interest in an activity is waning or that they are heading for a behavioral problem, you might try redirecting them to other areas of their interests by *positive suggestion.*   For example, you might say, "Alice and Mary, why don't you break out your matchbook collections and enter your new ones?" Be sure to have new and interesting activities such as games and arts and crafts projects in reserve for those inevitable nothing to do times. If you notice your two teenagers really getting into a heated fight again you might suggest to them "Let's walk." to cool things off. The child mourning a dead dog might be encouraged to express her grief in the form of a poem. A child threatening to hit you might be directed to pummel a pillow instead.

Discussion

This technique of offering substitute outlets has been found to work especially well with young children who are more easily distracted than older children, and who cannot be reasoned with as well. Offering a shiny spoon to an infant, for example, is an example of nonverbal suggestion.

It is interesting to note that chimpanzees often practice discipline by distraction in raising their infants. Instead of punishing an infant when troublesome, the chimp moms amuse the child by giving their undivided attention.

Rechanneling

Rechanneling, a form of positive suggestion that seeks more enduring changes in a child, refers to the encouragement of a child to express socially unacceptable impulses in substitute ways that are more constructive or socially acceptable. Basically it involves a sublimation of youthful energies and impulses.

It is truly surprising how many troublesome behaviors of children can be rechanneled into constructive, ego-building pursuits. The active, aggressive child, for example, can be encouraged to release his energy in such socially approved activities as physical contact sports (football, soccer, boxing), carpentry (hammering and sawing), drawing or painting, and playing the drums. Building and racing cars may provide a subsequent outlet for these energies. Scouting and club activities offer other constructive outlets. The child with compulsive habits (i.e., tendency to repeat the same behavior over and over or to impose a rigid order or arrangement on things) can be encouraged to perform tasks requiring care and orderly precision. For instance, the child might make model airplanes, or construct elaborate objects with matchsticks. These precision products will bring the child praise and also broaden his or her range of interests.

A youth who seeks excitement and independence by constantly running away from home could be allowed to visit relatives in a distant city by himself, attend a sleep away camp, or participate in a survival, back-packing hike in the wilderness. For rechanneling to be successful, it is obviously important to make the substitute activity as satisfying as the maladaptive one, and to offer a variety of outlets for the tremendous energies of youth.

MODELING

Whatever you would have your children become, strive to exhibit in your own lives and conversation.

Mrs. Sigourney

Parental Modeling

The most potent socializing force so far discovered appears to be children learning through observing what others do — particularly parents. Modeling refers to the example parents set for children by their daily *actions*. Children are the world's greatest mimics. They continually imitate what they see and absorb what they hear. Modeling can be more effective than language alone as it provides more meaningful nonverbal cues which provide a clear example to copy.

Most of what children know about socially-accepted ways of be-having they have learned through this process, i.e., imitating and ab-sorbing the behavior of their parents. This pervasive influence, then, tends to be more important than the more conscious, deliberate ef-forts of parents to teach and influence their children.

Accentuate Positive Behaviors

Mature parents will strive to set positive examples for their children in a variety of ways, including: facing daily problems with good judgment, common sense, and a willingness to accept the conse-quences of their actions; maintaining control over their emotions; applying themselves diligently to tasks and taking pride in their work; exhibiting an optimistic outlook on life; finding joy in present activi-ties rather than becoming overly concerned about past deeds or future projects; deepening their close, loving relationships; expanding their circle of friends and acquaintances; searching for additional knowledge throughout their lifetimes; and endeavoring to become more aware of the ideals and values which give meaning and direction to their lives.

Decrease the Negatives

Fears are extremely contagious. There is a considerable body of psychological literature which indicates that most of the fears of children are learned − either from their parents or from other children. Thus, if you readily reveal your fears in front of your children, e.g., fear of strangers, of the dark, of snakes, of big dogs, of heights, of dying, then the odds are greater that your children will acquire them by imitation. As far as possible, then, parents should summon up their courage and keep their fears under cover when children are around.

If you're not able to really conceal your fears, you should openly acknowledge them, e.g., "Gee, that scared us both, I guess." By admitting fears, you can strip away some of their sinister qualities and help relieve the obvious tension in children.

Apart from fears, you should try to control your negative atti-tudes, prejudices, and personal dislikes. If, for example, a mother has a negative attitude towards housework and continually complains while doing these tasks, there is a good chance that her children will develop an adverse outlook towards their household chores and possibly to work in general. Similarly, if a parent has a personal dislike for certain foods, that parent is well advised to keep these dislikes to herself.

In addition to keeping your fears, prejudices, and undesirable attitudes to yourself, you should also avoid using fear threats as a means of disciplining a child or even in jest. Examples of fear threats are:

The boogey man will get you if you do that.

There is a witch (monster) outside who will eat you if you ever talk to me like that again.

Something terrible will happen to you for that.

Discussion

Research shows that children are very aware of any discrepancy between what is morally right as told to them by parents and teachers and the actual behavior exhibited by adults. Thus, the wise parent will be particularly careful to avoid a contradiction of words and actions. Do you advocate honesty to your children while cheating a little on your income taxes? Do you preach responsibility while failing to keep your promises to children? Do you expect high academic achievement from your children while failing to show an intense interest in studying and learning yourself?

The "Do as I say not as I do" philosophy does not work well with children. As previously stated, the example you set by your actions is the most powerful teaching process in your home. It is much stronger than lecturing or preaching to children.

To increase the likelihood that children will imitate your positive behaviors, make an effort to display any positive feelings you may have towards these actions. For example, show the enthusiasm and interest you have for certain tasks by saying, "This is really fun and it is so easy!" In short, you can make an activity more appealing and attractive to kids when you make it seem enjoyable. The best teachers are the ones who are enthusiastic about what they are doing.

Children have more need of models than of critics.

Joubert

Modeling by Others

Although parents are by far, the most influential models in a child's life, children will also imitate other persons for whom they have respect, admiration, and/or affection. Thus, effective models for your children include older siblings, neighborhood friends, teachers, public figures, and fictional heroes. To assist your child in attending to these models, try pointing out features of the model's behavior that you want emulated. For example, you might observe, "Gee, your friend Maria always leaves promptly when her mother calls her!" Praising or rewarding a model for desired behavior in front of your child is another way to get your child to attend to the behavior.   Once your child exhibits the desired behavior, be sure to praise the act.

Television is a medium that has the potential to expose your child to considerable prosocial or antisocial modeling, particularly if your child is a heavy viewer, i.e., over four hours a day. There is a great deal of evidence now to indicate that you would be wise to monitor your child's viewing so as to minimize exposure to shows of violence and programs which are designed to produce fear or fright.

Discussion

In regard to prosocial modeling by others, it is noteworthy that a model can influence your child's behavior in two ways.

1. The model can engage in a behavior that your child has never experienced before and thereby induce your child to do something new, e.g., attend sleepaway camp.
2. The model can do something already familiar to your child and thereby induce your child to engage in this particular behavior rather than some other behavior, e.g., being respectful rather than discourteous to adults.

REWARDING

Jeremy Bentham(19th century) said that mankind has two masters, pleasure and pain. We tend to repeat those behaviors we find pleasurable and rewarding while avoiding those we find unpleasant. One of the most clearly established principles of learning is that if you want to increase a positive behavior in child then give the child something pleasurable following the performance of the desired act. Positive reinforcement refers to the rewards which follow behavior. These rewards can be classified as either primary (i.e., food, money, toys, and other concrete things or events) and secondary (i.e., social praise, attention, or recognition). The use of concrete rewards will be discussed here, while praise will be described as a separate technique.

Rewards can also be classified as either intrinsic (i.e., act which satisfies the child's goals or needs) or extrinsic (i.e., satisfaction or pleasure is derived from external sources). The long term goal in giving rewards is to substitute social or secondary reinforcers for primary ones, and then to develop an intrinsic rather than extrinsic source of reinforcement in a child. Apart from encouraging the repetition of a desired behavior, an additional expectation for the use of rewards is that they will make the child feel better about himself, and that in developing greater self-esteem he will acquire greater self-control. Rewards should also help build a positive relationship between parent and child since they represent, to some extent, love and esteem from an important person in the child's life.

There seem to be two legitimate ways of rewarding a child for desired behaviors. The first is to make the normal rewards or pleasant events in the home contingent upon the performance of actions expected of all. For example, you might tell the child that he can have no dessert until he has taken two bites of a new food on his plate, or no TV until his homework is done. Thus privileges are not made automatic, rather they are made contingent upon responsible behavior. An if this. . .then this (contingent) relationship is established between pleasant events in the home and unpleasant but normally expected behaviors. This has been called "Grandma's Rule," namely, *if* you eat your spinach *then* you get your dessert. . .first work, then play.

The second way of rewarding desired behavior is to give an extra reward for something particularly difficult for a child. If a child is terrified of the water, for instance, you might give a special treat for just accompanying the family to the beach; then for putting his feet in the water, and so on. In this way you may desensitize him to the feared situation. In addition, a slow starting child in school who has become discouraged with repeated failure might be offered a special reward for studying or raising his grades.

Guidelines

1. Concrete rewards should always be given in conjunction with social reinforcers, i.e., praise, affection, appreciation, individual attention. In this way the concrete reward can be gradually phased out and replaced with just the social rewards. Frequent use of both primary (tangible) and secondary (social) reinforcers helps create a positive orientation in the home, that is, a feeling that there are numerous rewards and satisfactions for appropriate participation in family life. In subsequent sections the use of social rewards will be discussed, i.e., praise, adult attention.

2. There are three general conditions for rewarding children. In the first case, you tell the child in advance that he will receive a reward only if he performs a certain desired behavior. In the second case, you say nothing in advance but give a reward after you notice a child performing the desired behavior. The third situation involves giving a reward for no specific behavior but just because you like the child or the way he generally behaves. The first condition is advisable when the child rarely if ever performs the behavior you desire because of low motivation, fear, or anxiety, or special difficulty. The second condition works well when you wish to increase the frequency of an appropriate behavior that already occurs with some regularity. The third condition is best when you want to show general approval or appreciation of the child's behavior.

3. Use anything the child likes as a reward — any high frequency behavior. Thus if your child likes to read but forgets to wash dishes, use "Grandma's rule" and make reading in the evening contingent upon washing dishes. If your child likes to eat

vegetables but not meat, make a portion of vegetables the reward for eating a portion of meat.

The more you know your children and their individual interests, likes, and activities, the more skillful you will be in finding effective rewards. Knowledge of child development is also helpful. For instance, candy has been found to be a more effective reward with 4–5 year olds than praise. Older children will not be motivated by food or games but will work for special privileges and extra money.

4. Be systematic in giving rewards. This means being specific, keeping records setting contingencies, and being persistent.

   a. *Specific.* Pick only one or two very specific, concrete, and observable behaviors to reward. Don't reward a child for some vague, global trait such as being good; rather reinforce more specific behaviors such as sharing his toys with others or sitting quietly in a restaurant.

   b. *Keep a record.* The more you monitor a child's progress by counting and making a record of the frequency of the desired act the more you will be able to note progress or lack of it.

   c. *Contingent.* Only give a reward after the child performs the desired action. But give the reward immediately after the act. Gold stars, points, or tokens exchangeable for more tangible rewards at a later date are one way of giving immediate reinforcement. Be consistent and reward every time in the early stages. Do not reward one day and not the next.

   d. *Persistent.* Regularly review your success or lack of it and revise your procedures as necessary, i.e., find a more powerful reward; try for a smaller behavior change. Don't give up!

5. A common error most of us make is to demand too much for too small a reward when we begin to teach something new to a child. The first little steps by a child need big rewards!

Discussion

One should not confuse a reward with a bribe. A reward is a compensation for good, meritorious, or desired behavior, while a bribe is a payoff for something illegal or wrong. Notwithstanding the studies of human motivation that have found positive reinforcers to be much more effective in producing positive behavior changes than such negative practices as nagging and punishing, some parents still feel it is wrong to reward a child for behavior that "is to be expected of him." In contrast to this rather strict, moralistic position (which tends to lead to harsh disciplinary measures), a more humanistic philosophy maintains that children (like adults) are entitled to be rewarded when they make a special effort to change, undertake a difficult task, or do something else of merit.

A pitfall to be avoided in using rewards is to fail to gradually fade them out in favor of social praise and, eventually, internal sources of self-satisfaction i.e., virtue and success are sources of rewards in themselves. Needless to say if you were to constantly reward everything a child does, you would run a high risk of raising a spoiled, manipulative child who would *only work for a reward.* As with anything else, rewards should be used with moderation and with knowledge of long term goals.

CONTRACTING

A contract is a formal, written agreement between parent and child. One type of contract specifies the terms concerning the rewards that will be given a child following his engaging in certain specific behaviors. The format and content of the contract is up to the discretion and ingenuity of the parents.

The following is a sample contract.

PERFORMANCE CONTRACT

I, John Adams, do hereby agree to wash the boat, keep the motor greased and make sure that all gear is treated and stored. These tasks will be done promptly after each use during the months of July and August. In payment, I will receive $5.00 per week — it being understood that this is half pay because I enjoy the boat too.

Signed _____
(child)

Signed _____
(parent)

Discussion

A contract is a useful tool with children because it makes your expectations and intentions about desired behavioral changes crystal clear. It is surprising the degree of ambiguity that exists in many homes as to what behavioral changes are desired of children and what the consequences will be for changing or not changing these behaviors. Contracts work particularly well when a child is capable of doing something but is just unmotivated and needs an added incentive.

A good contract will make reasonable and feasible demands of both parties so that neither feels taken advantage of or cheated. Thus, you would only use a contract when both parent and child are motivated to solve a problem and willing to do something different to resolve it. Often you will have to write a "reciprocal contract" with an older child, i.e., you agree to change your behavior, e.g., stop nagging, if he agrees to change his behavior, e.g., start attending school regularly. A good contract, then, is explicit and realistic in expectation, mutual in agreement, and flexible in the sense that it can be renegotiated whenever parent or child feel that the terms are unfair or unproductive.

Contracts can be initiated with younger children for simple household chores, e.g., feeding the cat, taking out trash. They not only teach children responsibility, but they reduce hassling and add needed structure to many households.

ADDITIONAL READING

DeRisi, W. J. and Butz, G.   *Writing Behavioral Contracts.*   Research Press, Champaign, Illinois, 1974.

SHAPING

Often the behavior you desire from your child is a rather big, complex task that is difficult to achieve all at once. Children tend to become discouraged when too much is expected of them in too short a period of time. They tend to learn slowly by taking small steps. It is often advisable, therefore, to break a complex task down into its component parts and to ask a child to perform only a small segment of the whole at first. Thus, rather than asking your child to perform the complex task of cleaning her room, you might ask her initially to put all the toys in her room in the toy box. The following week you might request that she also dust the furniture and window sills in her room. The next week you might ask her to vacuum the room as well.

By setting the difficulty level of tasks just below your child's felt competency, you ensure that the child tastes success immediately and regularly. This will, of course, nurture a child's self-esteem and self-confidence.

A related procedure is to reward your child for performing acts that are, at first, only remotely similar to your final goal. Suppose, for example, that you wish to have your child play cooperatively with others. First you would reward him for not teasing or being verbally abusive to his peers, then for sharing his possessions with others, then for playing by the rules of a game, and so on. This principle of *successive approximations* involves rewarding your child for behaviors that, at first, are only slightly related to your goal. Once the child learns these remote behaviors and they seem firmly established, you then reward behaviors that are successively closer and closer to the final goal. The point is you have to start somewhere and that somewhere may be quite a distance from the final goal when dealing with children. Shaping desired behaviors, then, requires considerable patience which is difficult for parents living hectic lives.

Discussion

In teaching young children new skills, e.g., combing hair by a four year old, you may first have to reinforce the attempt. Then reward a better attempt next time. In teaching a young child to tie his shoes you might initially reinforce pulling the strings tight; then pulling a string through one hole, etc. Reward the child with praise, attention, stars, toys (whatever is meaningful) for meeting each step towards the goal. If the child is unable to meet your request, return to the level where success can be attained. This only means that you are going too fast and must slow down.

By careful planning and execution, parents should be able to achieve step-by-step growth in a variety of new child behaviors, such as throwing a ball, table manners; and in eliminating unwanted behavior such as dawdling, and so on. The key is to think small and reward large. Usually we require steps that are too large.

CHANGING THE HOME ENVIRONMENT

Preventions of misdeeds are far better than remedies; cheaper and easier of application, and surer in result.

Tryon Edwards

An effective way of stopping many misbehaviors is to change the child's environment, as contrasted to efforts to change the child directly. Analogous to preventive medicine, environmental control means changing your household so that your child's disturbing behaviors are less likely to occur. The three main ways of altering an environment are to add to it, subtract from it, or rearrange it.

Adding to the home environment means making it more interesting, stimulating, and responsive to the child's needs. Bored, whiney children can quickly get involved in constructive activities if you have available a variety of materials such as clay, paints, puzzles, games, papers, etc. Music can also be used as a calming influence in the home. A playroom is also important where things are displayed so as to invite use and where children feel free to make a mess.

Reduction of environmental stimuli can prevent trouble as well, e.g., calming a child down by reading a story or turning on the TV. The period just before bedtime should be a calm, relaxing time for a child rather than a time of wild excitement or vigorous play. Child-proofing a house by removing all breakable, fragile, or dangerous objects from the reach of a toddler is another example of impoverishing an environment to prevent trouble.

By rearranging the schedule of daily events or simply using physical space differently you can avoid many conflicting situations between children. For example, if two of your children cannot be together for any length of time without fighting, try separating them physically (putting up a partition or divider in the play room, or imaginary line in the living room, or having them play in different rooms) or try rearranging their schedules so that they are not together (one does homework in the evening, one after school). If your child and your best friend can't stand each other, try rearranging your schedule so that your best friend only visits when your child is in school or in bed.

Discussion

An environmental or ecological approach can expand your perspective and conceptualization of a child's problem. Ask what it is in the home that is triggering off or maintaining the problem, and consider if some change (physical, schedule, or activity) could reduce the misbehavior.

PRAISING

> *Words of praise, indeed, are almost as necessary to warm a child into a congenial life as acts of kindness and affection. Judicious praise is to children what the sun is to flowers.*
>
> *Bovee*

In praising children you point out the worth of their traits, abilities, or achievements. *Praise* involves showing children you value and esteem their actions or efforts. As opposed to personal expressions of liking, approval or appreciation ("I like that!" or "Thank you for your help."), praise represents more objective feedback which validates the worth of a child's actions ("That was a thoughtful thing you just did."; "You really know a lot about science."; "You worked hard to clean your room."). Examples of nonverbal praise include making a scrapbook of a child's athletic achievements or prominently displaying diplomas or awards.

The educator John Dewey said that the deepest urge in human nature is the desire to be important. Praise gives children the needed sense of worth, competence, and confidence. This positive feedback is particularly important for inferiority-prone or shy children. When parents change their feedback from being primarily negative to being mostly positive a new atmosphere develops in the home. Interpersonal vibrations change and family members are drawn closer to one another. Somehow a child's ability to absorb failure and take risks increases.

Many parents feel funny giving praise for behaviors a child is "expected to do." When behaviors are taken for granted, however, the child either slows them down or performs them without enthusiasm and they die out. Parents appreciate a word of recognition from each other when they have worked long and hard around the house preparing a meal, cleaning the yard, fixing up a room, etc. Children, too, need to hear from others that their efforts and accomplishments are noticed and valued.

Descriptive versus Evaluative Praise

Haim Ginott, the noted child psychologist, once observed that "Direct praise of personality, like direct sunlight, is uncomfortable and blinding." Thus we should not praise a child's total personality ("You're a great kid!") but rather the child's specific behaviors. Ginott also recommended praising behaviors by making descriptive statements ("The colors in your drawing are so lively and happy!") rather than evaluative comments ("It's a terrific drawing!"). Direct evaluative statements tend to make people uneasy because they imply someone is sitting in judgment and that they will have the right to criticize you tomorrow. Also, when you use evaluative adjectives you have a tendency to exaggerate and make global generalizations ("You're so good!") which makes children feel uneasy or phony since they know they are not really that good. Statements which describe in a very specific way the commendable aspects of a child's behavior ("It takes a lot of strength to move that heavy workbench."), then, are more informative, realistic, and more apt to prompt self-praise. Research studies have verified the fact that young children show more positive changes in their behavior as a result of descriptive rather than evaluative praise. They seem able to draw positive inferences about themselves from descriptive comments about their behavior, i.e., they learn to praise themselves. Clearly, it takes both thought and subtlety to praise well.

Guidelines for Descriptive Praise

1. Vary the wording of your praise to avoid redundancy.
2. Be consistent in looking for behaviors to commend. If you rarely praised in the past, gradually increase your praise so that you do not sound phony to yourself or the child.
3. Praise is most effective when it is sincere and heartfelt. Also, give it with enthusiasm (with real feeling) rather than mechanically.
4. Try to establish eye contact with the child when you praise and deliver the compliment with a pleasant expression and tone of voice.
5. Praise is generally best given immediately, preferably while the child is still in the act. However, it is also effective to tell a child that you have been thinking about something he or she did a while ago and then give a compliment.
6. The following are examples of what to praise: age-appropriate play and task performance; obedience; cooperativeness and thoughtfulness to peers and siblings; remembering a chore; decrease in inappropriate behavior.
7. Freely give praise when it is due because of effort or achievement, but do not overuse praise by giving it for every little thing a child does.
8. If you have difficulty remembering to praise, try selecting five things about your child that you like even if minor (e.g., saying "Hello" when arriving home) — and praise the child at least five times during the next week. This will promote a change in your attitude, away from taking the child's behavior for granted.
9. Avoid spoiling praise by adding a negative comment, comparison, or habitual criticism, e.g. "That's good, now why didn't you do that before?" "Well, *finally* you've done it right!" (The child is made to feel stupid.)
10. The prime motive in giving praise should be the pleasure one feels in giving recognition to others. If, on the other hand, you use praise primarily as a method of making the child change his behavior, the child will sense this pressure and resist. A compliment differs from flattery in that it is objective and given without thought of gain; flattery is often mere lip service, or excessive praise given for ulterior motives.

Whenever you commend, add your reasons for doing so; it is this which distinguishes the approbation of a man of sense from the flattery of sycophants and admiration of fools.

Steele

As the Greek said, many men know how to flatter; few know how to praise.

Wendell Phillips

Promote Self-Evaluation

Another way to get your children in the habit of praising themselves after they have behaved well is to describe how good the act must make them feel. The following examples illustrate an attempt to foster self-evaluation in a child by imaginatively putting yourself in the child's shoes and expressing the feeling:

Looks like you had a good time painting that!
You worked hard on the poster and it must make you feel proud to gain recognition.
I imagine it was hard for you to tell the truth when your teacher was yelling so loud.
You really fixed that for me quickly. How did you think of doing it that way.

By giving positive feedback of this nature you not only let children know you are aware of their efforts and achievements but you are helping them become independent by reinforcing their own judgment and self-confidence. You are assisting children to develop an internal locus of evaluation that is realistic and verifiable.

Modeling Self-Praise

In order to create a family climate in which self-encouragement and self-praise are acceptable, try praising yourself in front of your children whenever you do something well or are proud of it. Since children learn best by imitation and modeling, they will learn to develop a positive attitude about their own accomplishments.

The use of this technique will be difficult because most adults have been taught that it is inappropriate to praise yourself or toot your own horn.

To begin using this procedure, practice self-praise internally, then vocalize praise of your work, and then move on to praising your personal qualities. You might explain to your children that you are praising yourself because you want to teach them how to be appreciative of their own efforts and qualities; that it is important for everyone in the family to value themselves and their efforts; that use of self-praise usually results in one performing desired behaviors more often in the future.

Noteworthy is the fact that research has indicated that self-praise and praise of others are positively correlated. It seems that one learns the general skill of praise-giving. It also seems logical that the more you can accept praise from yourself, the more comfortable you will be receiving it from others.

Summary

It is much more effective to use praise for positive behaviors rather than blame for negative behaviors to mold a child's character. Research studies have shown, for example, that when teachers praise less and criticize more, children misbehave at a higher rate. Criticism is a trap because although it temporarily stops a misdeed, in the long run it increases inappropriate behaviors because any form of adult attention tends to be reinforcing to children. As Will Durant reminds us: "Censure cramps the soul and makes the imperfect task forever hateful; praise expands every cell, energizes every organ and makes even the most difficult undertaking an adventure and a victory."

DID YOU PRAISE YOUR CHILD TODAY?

ADDITIONAL READING

Felker, D.W. *Building Positive Self-Concepts.* Burgess Publishing Co., Minneapolis, Minnesota, 1974. A complete description of the self-praise techniques.

PERSUADING

Thought convinces; feeling persuades.

Theodore Parker

Persuasion is a way of influencing children to do something by arousing their emotions, drives, and ideals more than their intellect. It's effectiveness derives from the fact that most of us are creatures of emotions, drives, and pride rather than reason. Compliance by children to persuasion is voluntary and based on their judgment that certain behaviors will inherently enhance their well-being. Like a good salesman, you must have a good knowledge of the basic wants and needs of people and the ability to see things from their point of view to make best use of this approach. Some specific persuasive strategies are as follows.

Making Verbal Appeals

An effective way to get a child to do something is to point out the positive aspects of that behavior. The advantage of the behavior for the child is highlighted by associating it with one of the child's needs, desires, emotions (e.g., joy, fear, envy, etc.) or values (e.g., to be good or to be grown-up). In other words, you induce a child to do something by talking about what the child wants and how this behavior relates to it, rather than talking about what you want or what the facts dictate. Rather than feeling pushed by you, the child feels pulled toward the behavior by its own attractiveness.

For example, you might appeal to the basic needs of the child (curiosity, joy, adventure, change): "This is fun and it's so easy."; "That looks like an exciting thing to do."; "You're probably tired of eating the same food all the time. This new dish will be a nice change from the ordinary."; "This book looks interesting. I always wondered what it was all about."; "John, I know making the football team means an awful lot to you. I think you'll find that if you eat everything on your plate you'll have the strength and energy to go full steam the whole game!"; "If you keep hitting other kids like that, nobody will want to play with you. You'll be so lonely."

You can also capitalize on the child's desire to belong and be accepted by others by using the bandwagon effect. You might say, for instance, "Jim, look at these statistics, hardly anyone is smoking pot anymore!" When children feel that everyone is doing it or not doing it, there is a tendency for them to want to jump on the bandwagon and join the crowd.

Parents should also appeal to the ego-ideals and values of the child (to be competent; be good). Since most young children want to appear grown-up and acquire status, you might try challenging them by saying: "This is probably too hard for you."; "You're probably not big enough to be able to do this yet." Other examples of appealing to the ego-ideals of the child are: "Is that the way an eagle scout would behave?"; "Charles, you've always been so smart and curious, especially in school. I wonder if the college you're interested in will be stimulating enough for you? It would be a shame to waste real intellectual talent like yours."

In making appeals, try to hook them into the child's emotions, imagery, desires, and personal values rather than calmly using reason to convince.

Dramatizing

Merely stating a truth usually isn't enough to convince people. Thus, a good advertising company will try to make a truth vivid (appealing to the senses and the imagination), and dramatic (use of dialogue). Moreover, a good ad man will make a truth come alive by the use of illustration, example, and testimonial. With these techniques in mind, you might want to show your child a color photograph of the lungs of a heavy smoker to induce him to stop smoking.

Rather than nagging your child to feed his dog, you might post a picture of a starving dog with a caption signed by the child's pet: "Please don't let this happen to me!" One picture can indeed be worth a thousand words. In lieu of lecturing the kids about bickering and fighting, you could try posting signs on the dining room mirror saying "Make peace not war!" "Brotherhood begins at home." or "Would you like to have yourself as a brother?" Also, you might want to leave around testimonials by a child's favorite athlete (e.g., the harmful effects of smoking).

You can try other novel means of capturing a child's attention, e.g., ring a cow bell to make an important announcement. Another effective way to arouse attention is to try to determine how the child expects you to react and do just the opposite. For example, rather than trying to calm a child down when he is in the midst of a temper tantrum, you could say, "Hey, that looks like fun." and stage a huge temper tantrum yourself. By being unpredictable and using surprise tactics, you can release tension, arouse children's interest, and inspire children to modify their usual way of responding (just as you have) or at least discuss possible new ways of solving problems.

"Buttering Up"

The selling power of "taking the client to lunch" is widely recognized in the business community. Moreover, research has shown that the extraneous gratification of eating while listening to appeals by others, increases the effectiveness of the appeals. Thus, try persuading your child to do something while he is eating. The power of primary reinforcers (food, sex) to modify human behavior is one of the most firmly established findings in modern psychology.

Another pregiving technique involves rewarding a child in one area prior to requesting his compliance is another. For example, you would first excuse a child from one of his daily chores and then tell him that you now expect him to study longer.

This technique also includes being as friendly, helpful, and pleasant as possible to a child in order to get him in a good frame of mind. Once he is in a positive mood, you would then make a request of him, e.g., to study, write a thank you note, etc. Children are especially skilled in being extra nice before they request a favor. Parents would be well advised to learn from their children how to apply this technique.

"Selling Up"

Typically, car salesmen first try to get you to agree to buy — perhaps a lower priced model or a stripped-down version — and then they point out how many other features you could get for just a few dollars more. Once you say yes the first time, subsequent yeses come a lot easier. So try giving easily-fulfilled requests to your child the first time, then give more difficult but the same type of requests. For example, you might first say, "Margaret, please put your Raggedy-Ann doll away." Later ask her to put more and more of her toys away.

When baking a cake first ask the child to come and help by pouring the milk in the bowl; once the child is there, you might ask for other assistance. In brief, you initially use a behavior that seems easy or attractive to get the child initially involved and then you gradually try to get the child to do other more complex behaviors.

CHALLENGING

As previously mentioned, a simple but useful way to motivate children to perform a task you desire or to give their best effort is to give a friendly challenge, such as, "I bet you're too young (too little) to do this!" or "Do you think you could build a bigger tower?" A challenge is effective when a child is clearly able to do something but is poorly motivated to attempt it.

You should, of course, be appropriately surprised, impressed, and pleased when your child accepts the challenge and accomplishes the task.

Preschool children, in particular, respond well to challenges.

The challenge aspect is often crucial for a child's growth. As the noted psychologist Piaget has pointed out, unless there is disequilibrium or imbalance between some aspects of a child's environment and himself, there will be no motive for change nor movement to a higher stage of development.

Another way of providing a developmental challenge is by proper grouping of children who are at different stages of development. Seeing other children perform tasks that he is capable of will stimulate the child to exert a greater effort to succeed. So apart from challenging a child to compete with himself, you can make constructive use of the competitive drive in every child. Thus, rather than directing your children to stop slouching at the dinner table, you could say: "Let's see who can sit the straightest?" Appealing to a child's competitive desire, to do as well or better than others, is an excellent way to motivate kids.

Discussion

Since American children have been found to be more competitive than children of other nations, competition must be used with discretion in this country. It should only be employed when winning or losing does not produce a great deal of anxiety. Competition can be used effectively to increase performance on simple, relatively unimportant tasks, such as stacking firewood, driving a golf ball, shooting pool, or developing good posture. It is particularly appropriate when there is no set criteria to evaluate individual performance, so that comparison with others is the only source of evaluatory feedback.

USING NATURAL CONSEQUENCES

An effective disciplinary procedure is to allow children to learn from the natural consequences of their behavior. The school of hard knocks can teach a great deal about life. As long as the natural result of a behavior is unpleasant rather than seriously harmful to a child you can let him learn for himself not to repeat the behavior. Children will learn for themselves that if they push somebody their size they will probably be pushed back, and that if they don't bother to study for a test they will probably receive a poor mark on it. They will also learn by themselves that if they walk barefoot on a hot pavement, their feet will regret it, and that if they eat too much popcorn and candy their stomach will invariably complain.

By standing back and permitting your children to learn from their mistakes, you will be fostering independence, self-reliance, and self-learning. Your children will see you as less negative and intrusive. So let your son walk to school if he dawdles and misses the school bus; if your daughter is 20 minutes late for dinner, let her eat a cold meal; if they spend their allowances too quickly, they'll have to wait until next week for treats.

Discussion

Teaching youths 12 years old and up to take the natural consequences of their misdeeds is the official policy of Families Anonymous (FA).

The parents of youths with drug, alcohol, and other problems simply refuse to bail their children out of jail, pay their fines, or show any sympathy when their child is sent to jail. The parents take the attitude, "We love you, but as we have told you repeatedly, we can no longer be responsible for your actions. You will always have a home and a family to return to, but you must learn to straighten yourself out — we can't do it for you." According to FA officials this is called "tough love" and it's tough to learn, but it works!

ADDITIONAL READING

Dreikurs, Rudolf. *The Challenge of Child Training.* Hawthorne Books, New York, 1972.

USING "GRANDPA'S RULE"

Excess generally causes reaction and produces a change in the opposite direction, whether it be in the seasons or in individuals, or in government.

Plato

At times, you will find it beneficial to satiate your child with an undesirable behavior before it becomes a habit. To *satiate* means to overindulge your children with more than enough of the behavior so that they become sick of it or disinterested as the result of fatigue or boredom.

Thus, when your child first says a curse word at home you might insist that he say it again and again and again until he is tired of it.

When your child first expresses an interest in smoking you might give him a cigarette and encourage him to smoke the whole thing by inhaling. While the child is still a little queasy from the first cigarette, you might recommend that he or she have another.

The famous "Grandpa's rule," in this regard, is that any child who wishes to smoke must first smoke five large cigars in succession. This usually produces a bored-and-weary or sick-and-disgusted reaction on the part of the child to a formerly attractive object. If your child refuses to go to bed, make a deal with him. Ask if he wants to stay up as late as you. If yes, keep the child up much longer than he really wanted. Then wake him up at the usual time. Repeat this procedure until the child learns not to stay up as late as parents do.

Discussion

Encouraging satiation does not mean you condone or recommend the undesirable behavior. You are simply encouraging your child to overdo so that all pleasure and desire is lost. . .at least temporarily. Be sure to encourage or insist upon satiation in a calm, friendly tone of voice. It may be necessary to repeat the overindulgence of the behavior several times after the initial effects wear off.

SUGGESTING

To know how to suggest is the art of teaching.

Amiel

To *suggest* means to bring a thought to a child's mind for considera-tion. It often leads to an action which the child otherwise would not have taken. A suggestion carries practically no pressure to comply so that the freedom to act or not is left with the child. The power of suggestion depends, in large measure, on the blind faith that most children have in the omnipotent figures in their world, e.g., their parents. Children tend to uncritically accept what their parents say as "the truth." This is particularly true if a positive relationship exists between parent and child.

Guidelines

A positive suggestion directs the child's thoughts to feelings and behaviors of a desirable nature. For example, a parent might suggest: "You're going to feel better after you take this medicine." or "You're very tired and will probably go right to sleep now." or "I know you're going to be very brave when you get the shot from the doctor."

A negative suggestion, on the other hand, directs a child's thoughts to undesirable behaviors. Try to be more aware of the times you give negative suggestions to your children, such as: "Well, girls don't do well in math anyway."; "John, you are going to drop that milk bottle."; "Stop playing with matches, you are going to set the rug on fire."; "You are a bad (naughty) child!"; "What are you, stupid or something?" When you give a negative suggestion you will find that almost invariably the undesirable behavior comes true.

Even more effective than a direct suggestion with an older child is an indirect suggestion, i.e., the idea is not obviously the product of another but appears to arise within the mind of the child himself. For example, you might say to your child, "John, from what you've said I gather that you feel the best way to settle this is for you to ask your sister to return your toy?" In this regard, suggestions that seem to strengthen ideas already present in a child usually produce action.

Also noteworthy is the fact that you can make a suggestion more effective by capitalizing on natural changes in a child's life development. For example, with an immature child, you might suggest that he will act more socially mature right after he has had a birthday or has gone away to camp.

Finally, physicians have long been aware of the power of suggestion to relieve certain psychosomatic disorders. A noted dermatologist, for example, reports that he often removes warts on children by having the child paint the wart with a harmless colorful dye while repeating this incantation:

> Every time I put this potion on, it is going to find the mother wart and the rest will die.

If the child openly believes in magic this technique almost always works in five to seven days. The power of this suggestion procedure seems to derive from two sources, an authority figure and the magical chant.

REQUESTING

All the sleeping dogs of pride are aroused against us when we give orders; at every imperative we stir up armies of defense. Ask and it shall be given you, command and you shall be refused.

J.E. Davis

A *request* means asking a child to do something for you as a personal favor. Children will readily comply with requests when you have a friendly, positive relationship with them. Examples of requests are: "I need your help on this very badly, will you do it for me?" or "I really have this 'thing' about long hair so will you cut it a little shorter as a personal favor to me?" Even very small children respond favorably to the pleasant request: "John, will you help me?" Requests come in two forms, direct ("Could you put out the napkins?"), and indirect ("Would you like to put out the napkins or shall I?")

Discussion

The difference between a request and an order is that when you make a request you are willing to accept a yes or no answer. Too often parents will tend to confuse a child by making a request when they are really giving an order or command. If a child has no choice in a situation make this clear by giving him a firm directive: "Mary, come to the table now!" rather than a request; "Would you like to eat with us now?"

Fortunately, parents can allow children freedom of choice in most situations and thus they can get in the habit of saying, "Please do this." rather than "Do this." This tends to foster cooperation in children and to create a positive home atmosphere. A responsible parent gives as few orders as possible but makes frequent use of requests, suggestions, and persuasions. By giving a child as many choices as possible you promote decision-making and prevent a child from feeling like a little robot who has little control over his life.

Reciprocity is extremely important in regard to requests; you must be willing to meet most of a child's requests if you expect him to comply with most of your's.

PROMPTING

There are numerous occasions in raising children when it is wise to cue or signal a child to either begin a desired behavior or stop an inappropriate action. Even adults like to be reminded about certain things, like dental appointments, overdue bills, etc. Also, people often need a period of preparation to make a transition from one activity to another. We know from physics that bodies in motion tend to stay in motion and bodies at rest will tend to stay at rest. To help your family overcome the laws of nature, give them a reminder so that they can get ready 5-10 minutes in advance of an event.

To help your children *remind themselves* what to do at certain times rather than your telling them what to do, ask the children to state what is expected of them, i.e., repeat the rule or expectation.

Verbal Prompts

Examples of verbal prompting are:

1. "Dinner in five minutes."
2. "Jimmy, what do you do at 5 o'clock?" (If child fails to remember, you state for him "Feed the dog.")
3. "Louise, do you recall our past discussion in which we came up with what to do now?"
4. "Joan, what is the rule when we are in the library?" (If child cannot remember, state: "No talking.") Most libraries have found it helpful to provide their own visual prompts, i.e., signs, of this rule.

Nonverbal Prompts

Among the silent, nonverbal signals you can give to prompt or cue your child towards desired behaviors are:

1. A motionless stance or one hand raised can mean attention is wanted.
2. A hand palm down and lowered by degrees can indicate the need for lowered voice or taking a sitting or lying position.

3. A finger in front of one's lips can signal "Quiet Please!"
4. Signs or checklists relating to desired behaviors can be posted on bulletin boards (effective with 8 to 12 year-olds).
5. To signal disapproval of a child's misbehavior you can use eye contact, facial frowns, hand signals, coughing, and body posture. Standing close to your child when he begins to act up is another effective technique. Sometimes it may be necessary to use physical contact, e.g., taking a child's arm and gently turning him around in his seat.
6. You might post or display around the home some printed evocative words such as *calm, patience, think.* These words trigger attitudes and call forth the quality they symbolize.
7. In one classroom where chewing gum was prohibited, the teacher gave reminders by sign language. She rapidly closed and opened her thumb and forefinger (imitating jaw motion) and then, like a baseball umpire calling out the runner, she motioned with her thumb towards the wastepaper basket! Other teachers have used as cues red lights which go on when a child is talking out of turn or otherwise acting inappropriately.

Discussion

Prompting or cueing should be distinguished from nagging which is a persistent unpleasant urging or scolding by finding fault. Prompting is a simple, noncritical, impersonal direction given when the child needs help in learning or when he needs a prod because of low motivation.

A prompt should be given only once or twice and:

As pleasantly as possible.
As privately as possible.
As calmly and matter-of-factly as possible.
As impersonally as possible. (What is the rule? What are you supposed to be doing?)

Keep using prompts until a young child's new behaviors are under control. Be consistent in the prompts you use, and praise compliance, while taking immediate disciplinary action if a child fails to respond to a prompt.

CONFRONTING (CALLING A PROBLEM)

Think not those faithful who praise all thy words and actions, but those who kindly reprove thy faults.

Socrates

Sometimes a parent will have a problem with a child's behavior which the child does not experience as a problem at all. For example, a child may have a habit of leaving toys or personal objects around for the parent to pick up. If you "keep in" your grievances toward a child, no matter how minor they are, you will accumulate inner anger and resentment that may eventually get out of control. Living with another person inevitably results in conflict. If the issues are never brought up there is no possibility of their being resolved.

The tendency to withhold bad news from others has been called the "mum" effect. In ancient times the bearer of bad news was often killed. Since bad news still arouses negative feelings, parents tend to overlook or water down confronting children when they cause problems. Nevertheless, an essential aspect of socializing children is to teach them the lesson of "reciprocity" i.e., all human relationships are based on mutual responsiveness to each other's needs and feelings. Children cannot just take, they must learn to be considerate of others.

Gentle confronting or calling a problem means telling children in a very clear way just how their behavior is causing you a problem and how you feel about the misbehavior. For instance, if your daughter has been neglecting to wipe her feet after it rains, you might say, "Jane, when you walk in the house with wet feet, it makes the floor a mess which means more work for me to clean up. This makes me quite annoyed." Notice that you have not only described in a very clear way the reason for your distress (more work), but you have also alerted the child to your negative feelings. You have not given an order or told the child how to solve the problem; rather you have left the responsibility for resolving the difficulty with the child.

A key to effective confrontation is a self-focus rather than other-person-focus. A self-focus means concentrating on expressing your own feelings and needs by means of *"I" statements*, e.g., "I really feel annoyed when you don't feed your pet as you agreed to do. This means more work for me." An other-person-focused confrontation results in a *"you" message* which tends to be fault-finding, threatening, or blaming in nature, e.g., "You really ought to be ashamed of yourself for neglecting your pet." or "How cruel you are to let your pet go hungry." or "You'll be sorry if you ever do this again."

In initial confrontations your emphasis is on teaching the child the specific reason you are distressed, e.g., "When you interrupt me like this I cannot finish what I have to say to your father." In later confrontations about the same problem you should stress more your escalating annoyance or anger, e.g., "I'm becoming really angry about your continuing to interrupt me!"

A basic assumption of the self-focused confrontation technique is that the child, being a reasonable person with good intentions, will resolve the problem once your disapproval is clearly brought to his or her attention in a straightforward manner. It further assumes that you have a close, positive relationship with the child so that a clear expression of your displeasure will motivate the child to seek to regain your goodwill. Until the child corrects the situation it should be made clear that there will be few if any positive interactions or favors from you in the near future. Generally, this form of mild punishment will influence children to correct misconduct on their own. If not, you will have to impose more severe penalties, such as loss of privileges.

Discussion

Confrontation should be used with caution and in moderation. Be sure your motive in confronting is to produce a positive behavior change in the child, not the desire to hurt back! After confronting, listen to the child to determine if there is a valid reason for the problem behavior. Maybe the child also has a need that is not being met, in which case you need to resolve this "conflict-of-needs" by discussion and negotiation.

To balance the use of negative "I" statements when you have a grievance, cultivate the habit of giving positive "I" messages when the child pleases you. A positive orientation to childrearing means you more often express your appreciation of children's behaviors than your displeasure. Rather than taking good behaviors for granted, you might say, "I really feel happy in playing this game with you."; "I like the way your face lights up when you are happy."; "I appreciate your help in getting ready for the party tonight."; "Thank you for cleaning up the mess in the kitchen as I asked." Appreciation is simply an expression of your personal approval of, or liking for, the child's behaviors, e.g., "I liked the way you jumped."; praise on the other hand is a more objective assessment of the worth of a child's behavior, e.g., "That was an extraordinarily long jump!"

ADDITIONAL READING

Gordon, Thomas. *Parent Effectiveness Training*. Peter Wyden, New York, 1970. Description of how to effectively confront children by using "I-Messages."

RESOLVING DISAGREEMENTS

The first duty of a wise advocate is to convince his opponents that he understands their arguments, and sympathizes with their just feelings.

Coleridge

An extremely valuable skill to teach your children is how to effectively resolve interpersonal conflicts by a logical argument or discussion rather than a quarrel. An argument lacks the intense hostility and resentment found in a quarrel. A *conflict situation* is one where there is a disagreement between two people because of a specific issue or event. Both have grievances that must be worked out. The hallmark of a mature conflict-resolution attempt is a calm, rational, open discussion of the issues, i.e., a problem-solving emphasis rather than personal attack or criticism. Both parties should focus on explaining what needs of theirs are not being met as well as listening to the needs and views of the other person. The intent of the meeting should not be to hurt, blame, or win but to understand and help seek an equitable solution. There should be a spirit of cooperation, mutual acceptance of responsibility or fault, and mutual trust rather than anger or blame. Moreover, the conflict will more likely be re-solved if each party demonstrates an open mind rather than a closed, know-it-all attitude.

In a dispute between two of your children, you will most likely have to assume the role of arbitrator or peace-maker, and model these mature approaches to settling conflicts. The following proce-dure may assist you in helping children, especially older children, resolve their differences. You will, of course, be more effective in your arbitrator role if you have previously modeled these procedures in your own efforts to resolve conflicts with other members of the family. The procedure is as follows:

1. Ask each child to briefly state his views and explain what needs of his are not being met. Rather than raising their voices, the chil-dren should be trained to speak softly and control their anger.
2. Help them to note any points of agreement.
3. Note the points of disagreement in a clear way and ask if the children agree that these are their differences of opinion.
4. Summarize the disagreements and explore for deeper causes of difficulty.
5. Ask both parties to offer tentative solutions to the conflict and list them.
6. Encourage the children to select a solution they consider best in terms of meeting the needs of all concerned.
7. Get the children to agree on ways of implementing the solution.

One phase of the conflict-solving process that seems particularly crucial in stage five — solution finding. An effective solution finding technique that can resolve many conflicts is the use of compromise. Compromise means that you resolve the conflict by finding a com-mon ground acceptable to both sides. In a compromise situation, both parties agree to give up some of their demands and make con-cessions. By this *quid pro quo* procedure, parents can avoid the typi-cal power struggle with their children which inevitably ends up with someone becoming a loser. To illustrate a compromise, a parent might allow his son to wear his hair exceptionally long if he agrees to wash and comb it regularly. A compromise solution is a particularly appropriate technique to use with teenagers since it involves the use of reason rather than force.

In using the conflict-resolving procedure, it is very important that the time be right, i.e., both parties are calm, unhurried, and willing to attempt a resolution. It is also important to teach children to attempt to resolve conflicts as soon as possible rather than living with their resentment for weeks or months.

Discussion

By mediating conflicts in this manner you indicate to your children that you respect and have confidence in their ability to resolve interpersonal difficulties in a mature, rational manner.

Also, you will find this procedure helpful when there is a legitimate conflict between your needs (e.g., for quiet) and the needs of your child (e.g., for making noise while he plays). These conflicts are best settled in the manner previously described, i.e., listen to the needs of the other person; express your needs in an honest, straightforward, nonblaming way; and then explore solutions until you find one that is mutually satisfying.

Usually in a conflict situation wherein there is a difference between what a child wants and what you want, you think of someone winning (you) and someone losing (child). You tend to think of either being strict (parent wins) or being permissive (child wins). A third solution which is described in detail by the psychologist Tom Gordon is a "no lose" method of conflict resolution wherein you ask the child to join you in a search for a solution acceptable to both of you.* Since the child is an active participant in this process – and the emphasis is on the fact that *we* have a problem – he or she is less likely to try to undermine it at a later date. For example, you might say, "Joan we seem to have a problem here. Your room is so messy that when I go to get your dirty laundry I really have to search and it's a lot more work for me. We need to look for a solution to this that we can both live with."

Conflict resolution wherein emotions are kept under control, the focus is on searching for solutions rather than finding fault, and the goal is for both sides to win rather than for one person to dominate the other is a skill that needs considerable practice lest the session

*Gordon, Thomas, *Parent Effectiveness Training.* Peter Wyden, New York, 1970.

become a battle in which the individuals try to convince each other that they are right and the other wrong. You have to cultivate the spirit of mutual trust and caring which must prevail for this technique to be successful.

Remember that disagreement always goes better against a background of praise. Be sure to balance your disagreements with common ground that you agree on and things that you like about the child. Finally, never attempt to resolve conflicts when one or both parties are emotionally upset. Allow a "cooling off" period for both parties to think it over.

DISTANCING

Since much of children's misbehavior is directed towards obtaining parental attention, try leaving the scene of the children's disturbance for a while.

When you feel you are rapidly approaching the end of your patience, for example, retire to the bathroom or bedroom and lock the door. You will often find that the disturbance dramatically ends when you do this and that the children were quite able to cope with the situation themselves. A temper tantrum, for instance, is no fun unless there is an audience. It is also very difficult to continue complaining or whining when no one is listening. Distancing would not be used, of course, when there is real danger of a child causing harm to himself, to others, or to property.

Arranging for someone to watch the kids for a while is another way to find needed relief when you feel about to lose your patience with them.

Discussion

More extensive forms of parent-child distancing, e.g., a child attending summer camp, visiting relatives, or living at a boarding school, are sometimes effective in relieving explosive parent-child conflict situations.

Parents also need to get away. Wasting an afternoon by yourself and spending weekends or vacations without the children can help restore psychological equilibrium. It is unhealthy to be on duty all the time in any job. Some parents arrange to have a date with each other once a week and regularly schedule a babysitter for the children. This not only helps them relax but keeps their romance alive. Brief or extended vacations are especially important for parents who wish to avoid becoming "burnt out" in the parenting role after periods of severe crisis or extended stress. It is important to be able to spot the early warning signs of becoming psychologically run down, i.e., irritability and impatience, feeling the "blues and blahs," sleeplessness, increased proneness to accidents and illnesses, difficulty controlling hostile outbursts, hypersensitiveness to criticism, decline in your socializing, and inability to relax or enjoy yourself.

ESTABLISHING ROUTINES

Traditions, customs, habits, routines are all the arrangements which make everyday life self-starting and self-regulating.

Eric Hoffer

Children thrive best on order and regularity. They are happier when they know what to expect. By setting up regular, unchanging procedures for conducting daily events, parents provide an environment that is both dependable and predictable. To an immature child, a predictable world is a safe world, free of confusion and uncertainty. Routines also promote efficient learning by supplying a script of expected actions. They prevent disorganized, chaotic households.

Daily routines should be carefully set up and consistently carried out for such regular events as bedtime, wake up time, meal times, toilet times, chore times, free play times, play time with daddy, or for the older child, homework time.

A bedtime routine might consist of one hour of quiet TV watching, followed by a prompt ("Five minutes till bedtime, dear."), bathroom visit, bedtime story, and then lights out. The same sequence would be conducted every night starting at the same time. No nonsense, stalling, or arguing by the children would be tolerated.

Guidelines

1. Be flexible and change your routines regularly — even daily at times — to meet changes in the activities of your family, and developmental changes in your children. Bedtimes, for example, must be adjusted to the age of the child.
2. Rather than bossing or nagging, try posting the daily routines on a bulletin board. In this way the kids will do most of their grumbling at the posted schedule, not at you.
3. Allow few exceptions to a routine because exceptions are the source of problem situations and uncertainty. The only exceptions should be for extraordinary events or real emergencies. Otherwise the routines will seem to be governed by your personal whims or fancies.
4. Your attitude towards a routine should be impersonal and unemotional, but interested. It should be clear to a child that it is his or her responsibility to conform to a routine, not your's.
5. Make it clear which of the daily routines are requirements that will be enforced.

Discussion

The quiet execution of ordinary routines of daily living is the earliest form of discipline for children. While all children need routine, this structure is particularly important for hyperactive, impulsive, slow-learning, and anxious-fearful children.

Despite the obvious value of routines for teaching self-discipline to children, many parents find it difficult to implement fixed schedules for various reasons, such as personal disorganization, preference for "free-living," or fear of becoming too rigid and controlling. Unfortunately children raised in homes with fluid schedules find it difficult to adjust to the fixed routines of school and business, e.g., a 9 to 3 school day with clearly scheduled events. Apart from other considerations, then, implementation of daily schedules is simply good habit training.

Habit is the beneficent harness of routine which enables silly men to live respectably, and unhappy men to live calmly.
George Eliot

SETTING LIMITS (RULES AND REGULATIONS)

One of the most important functions of parenting is to control children's behavior by means of rules and regulations. It is also one of the most difficult aspects of childrearing since it seems much easier not to enforce a rule than to hassle with kids about it. Also, adults tend to fear that children will no longer like them if they have to restrict the children's behavior. In the long run, of course, children will like, and even more importantly, respect you more if you provide them with the structure they need to develop inner controls and self-discipline. Apart from depersonalizing conflicts, i.e., it is not you against the child, but the child's specific behavior against a rule, rules have the advantage of clarity, advance notice, consistency, and fairness (apply equally to everyone). We all must learn to live within rules and limits so that an orderly group process can be maintained. Studies have shown that it is possible to be firm and demanding with children, while still being affectionate and warm with them. An appropriate balance between control and affection is needed for children to grow up well adjusted.

Any demand made on a child is a rule. A long-term rule is one that must be enforced again and again over a long period of time, e.g., "Make your bed every morning." A short-term rule or command is a spontaneous directive given a child about a particular situation, e.g., "Don't make those loud noises!" The following guidelines are offered with a view towards assisting you to be more effective in setting limits with children.

Guidelines

1. *Give Sparingly.* You will be more effective if you set only a few household rules, i.e., three or four. Not only will children remember them better but it is just not possible for you to enforce a large number of limits. It is better to enforce five rules 100 percent of the time than ten rules 50 percent of the time! Most parents and parent-surrogates set too many limits and don't enforce any of them consistently. So be sure that all your

rules are important and essential for harmonious living. Studies have shown that the more you increase your rules and commands, the more opposition you will receive from your children. Allow children the opportunity, then, to learn from the natural consequences of their behavior, i.e., if they hit a bigger sibling, they will probably get hit back.

2. *Be Clear and Be Specific.* State the limit in a crystal clear manner and forceful tone of voice. Avoid vague, subjective directions, e.g., "Your clothes must look nice before you can go out." What does "look nice" mean? It will probably mean different things to you and a child. If a rule is clearly stated, a child will instantly know when he has broken it, e.g., "Every day your chore is to empty the trash. This means the baskets in the kitchen, bathroom and laundry room. This must be done before you go to bed." Be succinct (the less talking the better), and impersonal in stating rules. Thus, don't say, "I want you to stop riding your bike in the house," rather say, "Bike riding outside, not in the house." Say, "It's bedtime!" not "You go right to bed!" Don't give a direction by asking a question, e.g., "Would you like to come in now?" If the child has no choice in the matter, be honest by giving a clear *order,* not a *request* which implies a choice.

3. *Set Reasonable Rules.* In making a demand on a child be sure that he is physically or developmentally able to do it, e.g., mow the lawn, and that you are not infringing on his needs for rest, relaxation, and study. Being reasonable also means being tuned in to the present emotional and physical state of the child. Studies show that children who are tired, hungry, ill, or emotionally upset, are less likely to comply with parental commands. Thus, minimal demands should be placed on children at these times. The more legitimate your command, i.e., involves the needs or rights of others, the more obedience you will get, especially by adolescents. Also, children will obey rules more readily when both you and they benefit from the rule. If only you or other adults derive benefit from the rule, you can expect more resistance to the rule.

Another aspect of being reasonable is not to set too high a standard of performance. Consider the age of the child and his present way of looking at things. A neat room may just not be important to a teenager. Rules should not be used as your way of imposing your values on a child, e.g., cleanliness, quiet, neatness. You can avoid many battles if you learn to accept different standards in some activities.

4. *Consistently Enforce Rules.* Before giving a directive, be certain you can enforce it consistently. Throw out any rule you do not intend to enforce 100 percent of the time. Ask yourself if you will know every time a child breaks the rule, without relying on someone else's testimony or surveillance. Consider if your spouse will enforce the rule as consistently as you. Follow the three step approach to enforcement: 1) Set a time limit for completion of your directives. Make the end of the time limit an event in which the child usually participates, e.g., a child's bed must be made before he goes to school in the morning. 2) Ensure the task is carried out. This involves preventing the child from participating in a customary event, e.g., going out to play, until the task has been completed. 3) Recognize the child's feelings. Children inevitably test a new rule and tend to give you protestation, complaints, and other emotional reactions. Allow your children to express their feelings and assist them to be in touch with themselves by recognizing them yourself, e.g., "You really want to go to the movies tonight and feel angry that it's against the rule on school nights." While showing concern for the child's feelings and desires, you should avoid getting into an argument with an emotionally upset child about the necessity of the rule itself. Such arguments are fruitless. Explain the reason for the rule once (or twice for a young child) and then ignore any further protestations from the child.

Being firm means you allow a child to break or bend a rule only on the rarest occasions that border on emergency situations, such as sickness. It means ignoring any other objections and excuses. Simply tell the child that he or she knows the rule and that you will accept very few excuses. Stick to your guns!

Remember that child development research has clearly shown that the most well-adjusted children come from homes where parents clearly define limits and express explicit expectations which they firmly and consistently enforce.*

5. *Prescriptive Wording.* Try to express your command in a positive way, i.e., place more emphasis on telling the children what to do (prescriptive) rather than what not to do (proscriptive). Thus, you might say, "Talk in a quiet voice" rather than "Don't shout." or "Blocks are for building things, not for throwing." In this way you are teaching children the acceptable way of doing things.

6. *Give a Leeway.* Since children, especially younger ones, find it difficult to change their ongoing activity, give them a fore-warning about a time limit. In other words, if you want them to come in from play, allow them a few minutes to finish playing by saying, "Five minutes more, then come in."

7. *Establish Reciprocity.* Children are more likely to obey you when you have a close relationship with them and they feel that you have been very attentive to their needs and requests, i.e., there is reciprocity in the relationship in that you both readily comply with each other's requests and are tuned in to each other's needs. You can expect considerable rebelliousness in a one-sided relationship wherein children feel they have to comply with many restrictions while no one seems to be sensitive to their needs.

8. *Expect Compliance.* There is a tendency for adults to get what they expect from children. If they expect children to be good and obey reasonable rules, they most likely will get compliance. Most of the time children do obey adult directives – especially from parents. Even during the first year of life, for instance, studies have shown that infants comply 67 percent of the time to their mother's commands. Even during the "terrible two's," children show a similar compliance rate. Also, the more positive your own attitude is toward law and authority, the more positive will be the children's.

9. *Prime the Pump.* Children are more likely to obey a big request from you if they have done some similar smaller favors for you.

---

*Smith, J.M. and Smith, D.E. *Child Management.* Ann Arbor Publisher, 1964. A more detailed account of how to enforce rules.

For example, a child will more readily set a table if he had previously been responsible for putting the dinner plates out.

10. *Allow Children a Choice and Voice.* The more children have participated in setting up a rule, and the more they all agree the rule is necessary and sensible, the more they will readily comply with it. Thus, family council meetings are advisable wherein the youngsters are encouraged to express their opinions about a difficulty and help to resolve it by establishing a rule. So give children experience in decision-making and in regulating their own behavior.

11. *Periodic Review.* Families should sit down together on a regular basis to review their rules with a view towards making necessary changes. As children grow older, there should be a need for fewer and fewer rules. Discuss the rules together and make compromises as needed. The few you feel strongly about should be enforced no matter what other parents are doing.

12. *Prompts.* The next time your child forgets a rule, don't remind him, rather ask, "What's the rule about slamming doors?" Have the child state the rule in its entirety. After a few lapses, the child should remember and obey.

13. *Praise.* Be sure to smile and praise children for following the rules. Use a child who adheres to a rule as a model by publicly announcing to the family why the child is being praised.

14. *Feedback.* If your command or directive is complicated or your child is young, check to see if the child understands by asking for feedback. e.g., "What are you supposed to do?"

15. *Give a Choice.* Directives which allow a child some freedom of choice tend to result in less opposition. Thus, instead of telling a child, "Put that food back.", you might say, "You can either put some of the food back in the bowl or on my dish, whichever you prefer."

16. *Promote Self-Regulation.* Sometimes it is better to ask a question rather than give a directive. Thus, you might say, "Karine, what are you doing?" This will serve as a signal to the child that the behavior is not only inappropriate, but that you are aware of it. It also indicates that you expect the child to remedy the situation.

If a child is directly bothering you, you might explicitly tell him so and state how the behavior is interfering with your needs.

If the child cares for you at all, he or she will tend to correct the situation spontaneously without the need for an order or solution from you. Remember the first guideline — the fewer orders you give the better.

17. *Make a Plus out of a Minus.* Try making a yes response when you would ordinarily give a no. Thus, if your child asks to do something not appreciated by you at that particular time or place, suggest an alternative. For example, you might say, "Yes, you can play with your toy when dinner time is over." rather than "No, you can't play now!"

18. *Requests.* Don't give a command if a request (e.g., "Please rest for a while.") would do as well or better — as they usually will. Infrequent use of commands helps a child avoid the sense of being "bossed around." The more responsive you have been to a child's requests, of course, the more readily the child will comply with your requests.

19. *Gradually Reduce.* Ideally, as children grow, the limits on their behavior are gradually lessened; they should experience increased autonomy. Unfortunately, for many children the pattern is a long period of rules and regulations and then an abrupt change into independence. When many teenagers go off to college or to work, they are expected to achieve instant adulthood, without a transitional period of gradually expanding responsibilities and decision-making.

20. *Confidence.* Be certain you are right in setting a limit. If you are uncertain, feel guilty, or lack confidence in yourself the child will sense this and balk at complying. When children detect ambivalence or guilt on your part they will attempt to sway you by stubbornness or sympathy-seeking.

Use of Parental Authority

Where love rules, there is no will to power; and where power predominates, there love is lacking. The one is the shadow of the other.
Carl Jung

To be comfortable regulating children you must be secure in the role of an authority figure. *Authority* means the power or right to give commands, enforce obedience, take action, or make final decisions. Effective authority is based on superior knowledge or expertise and is administered within an atmosphere of love and respect. The aim of parental authority is not to curtail freedom but to give a child freedom of judgment and action within manageable limits. As an authority, you should be both permissive and restrictive and strive to achieve a balance between the two.

In our permissive, "freedom oriented" society, many adults have unfortunately become uncertain and guilt-ridden about using their legitimate authority. The constructive use of authority is an essential function of childrearing. Children want and need guidelines as to what *is* and *is not* socially acceptable behavior. They need to learn that freedom does not mean a license to do whatever you please; that individual freedom is limited by the responsibility to respect the rights of others. Contrary to the philosophy of Rousseau, children are not noble savages that should be left alone to unfold as flowers. They need parental guidance and limit-setting to become socialized.

The foundations of parental authority are threefold:

1. *Legal.* By law you are given authority and responsibility to supervise your child so that he or she behaves in a socially acceptable way.
2. *Power.* You control most of the resources in the home (money, food) and you possess superior strength — at least during the child's early formative years.
3. *Expertise.* You have superior knowledge, experience, and competency which gives you natural authority. Just as children naturally look up to athletic coaches, they should respect your expertise on how to live in a society. Children learn respect for authority from the superior wisdom and strength of character they see exhibited by their parents. Children must see that you are not only wiser, but tougher, braver, more strong-willed, than they are.

Although no parent consistently uses a single approach, psychologists have found that parents can be classified into one of four styles of exercising authority.

1. *Dictators.* Parents who tend to espouse a dictatorial approach and stress authority and blind obedience. They follow a strict

authoritarian approach and tend to say no a lot. Their children tend to be inhibited, fearful, and conforming.
2. *Appeasers.* Parents who tend to be predominantly conciliatory and who give in to the child at crucial times. They seem to be afraid to enforce limits so that their children often get what they want. In an effort to avoid trouble, these parents tend to avoid issues and try to circumvent problems and confrontations. Children raised in this permissive atmosphere are prone to maintain an infantile life-style and enter adulthood expecting immediate gratification of their impulses.
3. *Temporizers.* Parents who tend to vary their approach in accord with the situation. If the situation is pleasant they tend to be pleasant. If a situation tends to get out of control these parents become confused and uncertain. Lacking a firm philosophy of childrearing, they follow no consistent pattern of parenting.
4. *Cooperators.* Parents who are mostly friendly and interact with children on a basis of mutual respect. They will say yes or no to a child depending on the child's stage of development and what can reasonably be expected of the child. They try to give as much freedom of choice as possible but are comfortable setting limits when necessary. Other terms for this approach include "informed permissive," "democratic," and "authoritative."

Authoritative, according to the psychologist Baumrind, means parents who have high respect for their children and for themselves, who present clear goals and standards of behavior for their children, and who guide their children as loving and reasoning experts while at the same time allowing their children much leeway in behavior and choices.* Research studies conducted to date have indicated that the authoritative approach is the one most likely to result in children who are both autonomous and socially responsible.

In conclusion, the American philosopher Thoreau once aptly defined the most important lesson you, as the authority figure, can teach your child:

> *Raise your child so that he will make himself do what he knows has to be done, when it should be done, whether he likes it or not. It is the first lesson that ought to be learned, and however early a man's training begins, it is probably the last lesson he learns thoroughly.*

*Baumrind, D. "Current patterns of parental authority," *Developmental Psychology* 4: No. 1, Part 2, p. 103, 1971.

WARNING

If your child persists in his noncompliance of a rule or command, before imposing a penalty give a warning signal. The warning should only be given once and should always be followed by a specific unpleasant consequence when ignored. So do not give vague threats ("You'll be sorry if you keep that up.") or doomsday statements ("You'll have your head handed to you if you don't stop!"). Rather, give a clear, realistic warning which consists of two parts: (1) a statement of the misbehavior and (2) the consequence that will certainly be administered if the child continues to misbehave.

> "This is a warning. If you use that word again, you will have to go to your room for five minutes."
>
> "I've asked you to stop teasing your sister. If you do it once more, you'll have to go to your room."
>
> "Joel, I'm not going to tell you this again. Either stop complaining or we're going to leave the restaurant. It's your choice."

Discussion

Be sure your tone of voice is firm and carries a negative inflection. Your voice quality — like your message — should be both assertive and disapproving. Otherwise, the child will be confused because your words will say one thing and your tone of voice another.

For effective warnings, the negative consequence should be consistently and immediately administered. If the misdeed is a frequent occurrence, omit the prompt and warning and immediately impose the penalty.

If you want your child to trust and respect you, then you should give warnings rather than threats. A warning is a realistic statement of an imminent penalty; a threat is an exaggerated statement of possible harm which is designed to intimidate a child, e.g., "You're going to get killed if you keep that up!"

IMPOSING PENALTIES

> *Of nineteen out of twenty things in children, take no special notice;*
> *but if as to the twentieth, you give a direction or command, see that*
> *you are obeyed.*
>
> Tryon Edwards

Punishment means imposing a penalty for a wrong-doing. The penalty must be unpleasant to be effective and thus involve some type of loss, pain, or suffering. Since the word punishment has acquired considerable adverse connotations (retribution rather than correction; harsh punitiveness), *imposing penalties* seems a better title for this method of discipline. Applying an unpleasant consequence for a child's misdeeds is probably the most controversial topic in childrearing and the one which makes parents feel most uneasy.

The short range goal of imposing penalties is to stop the misbehavior; the long range goal is to teach and motivate children to stop misbehaving on their own, i.e., be inner-directed. Children want to be corrected, but they want correction within a general spirit of helping and caring for them. By enforcing a rule, you help children learn their boundaries and thus establish inner controls. Do not feel guilty about imposing penalties on occasion. It is not only a form of love to enforce limits when they are needed, but it is a necessary part of the socialization process for a child.

Penalties are most needed when the misdeed is serious in nature (harmful to self or others; open defiance of parental authority, i.e., "I won't do it.") or very frequent. The defiant child who throws down the gauntlet and says, "I will not! You can't make me!" particularly needs to lose the power struggle. This is one situation you absolutely must lay down the law if you are to maintain authority and be in charge of your home. Parents who are prone to be permissive and to give in to problem children should read Dr. James Dobson's book, *Dare to Discipline.* *

Apart from the certainty of penalty, a key to effective discipline is to make your penalties reasonable. In depriving a child of something

---

*Dobson, James. *Dare to Discipline.* Tyndale House, 1970.

or in requiring restitution, be sure that the penalty you impose is logically related to the misdeed — both in type and magnitude. The nature of the misconduct should determine the penalty, not your personal preference or whim. This is an important principle since one of the most common questions parents ask about discipline is how do I enforce limits in such a way that my child will accept the penalty and view it as reasonable? Once children see the logic behind the penalty, they can accept it better — it seems more natural, reasonable, and objective. By giving children the freedom to make choices about how to behave, you have the right to expect them to face the logical consequences of their decisions. Rather than assigning penalties or consequences arbitrarily, make them directly related to the misdeed.

A logical penalty should first of all be proportional to the offense in degree of severity. Thus a teenager who misses a curfew should not be grounded for two months. This is overkill which breeds ill will and resentment because of its injustice. Nobody likes to live for two months with a penalty hanging over their head. Strive for a balance between the magnitude of the misdeed and the penalty. Penalties should never be so mild as to be inconsequential nor so strong as to be devastating or immobilizing. If a penalty is excessive, the children will focus on your unfairness rather than on their role in the act. So avoid trying to eliminate a misdeed "once and for all" by overdoing the penalty.

Secondly, the type of penalty should be related to the type of offense. For example, if a child cannot act in a socially acceptable manner with others in the home, he should be socially isolated for a period until he can behave appropriately with others. If a child leaves toys around, he should not be allowed to play with anything else until the toys are picked up. If a child rides his bike without permission, he should lose the privilege of bike riding for one day.

It is clear that penalties must be planned ahead. In the "heat of the moment" it is very difficult if not impossible to determine reasonable penalties. When emotions are high there is a tendency to generate a "lot of heat but not much light" on a problem.

Further examples and a more complete discussion of the concept of logical consequences can be found in Rudolf Dreikurs' book *Logical Consequences.* *

*Dreikurs, R. and Grey, L. *Logical Consequences. A New Approach to Discipline.* Hawthorne Books, New York, 1968.

Types of Penalties

There are three main types of penalties one can apply after a misdeed: 1) make the child perform an unpleasant act; 2) deprive the child of something pleasant; or 3) inflict psychological or physical pain on the child.

1. *Child Performs Unpleasant Act (Restitution).* Apart from requiring the child to do extra work unrelated to the misdeed, you can have the child make restitution or amends for the act. The goal of this "victim-centered" form of discipline is to direct the child's attention to the plight of the victim of the act. Undoing or making amends for your wrongdoing teaches the harmful effects of your misdeed on the victim and encourages you to imagine yourself in the other person's place. Penalties which represent concrete acts of reparation help the child learn that when you hurt someone, you should do something to make it right again. Restitution, then, is an altruistic rather than punitive form of discipline. Studies of altruistic discipline have found it to be related to other acts of altruism in children. Rather than just paying a penalty which is unrelated to the misdeed — thus wiping the slate clean in some children's eyes and freeing them up for repeating the offense — restitution seems to help develop a feeling and caring about others.

   Examples of restitution are: making a child apologize after he has teased or insulted a peer; having a child pay to replace a toy he has broken; and requiring teenagers to clean up a school building and playground after an act of vandalism. Of course, if children refuse the opportunity to make restitution, another form of penalty will have to be imposed.

2. *Deprivation.* To deprive a child of pleasant experiences you can either take away privileges and possessions or send the child to a "time-out" area.

   (a) *Loss of Privileges or Possessions.* Loss of TV watching privileges, driving the family car, no desserts or treats are examples of frequent penalties imposed by parents when children break the rules. Some families also give the "silent" treatment to a rebellious child. This means no family member will talk to or interact with the child until he or she conforms to the rule.

(b)   *Time-Out (TO)*. Requiring a young child to go to a quiet area after annoying other family members is often a good strategy to help the child regain control and to allow tempers to cool off. Thus, a time-out means the child leaves the scene of a misdeed and goes to a quiet place elsewhere in the house to do nothing until allowed to return. The TO area should be devoid of interesting things to do or look at, e.g., select a stairway or bathroom. The TO area should be far enough away to prevent any further occurrence of the misbehavior yet close enough for the child to hear what he is missing.

Some Do's and Don'ts for Time-Out:

1.   Remember to give a warning first that TO is imminent unless the annoying misbehavior stops. For example, you might say, "Joan, you will have to take a time-out if your silliness at the table continues. You can either stay here and act appropriately or leave. You decide."

2.   Tell the child to go to the TO area if the misbehavior continues. If the child resists leaving, use the minimum physical force necessary to enforce the departure to TO. Ignore protestations on the way and give no further attention while you escort the child.

3.   Tell the child that you will say when TO is over. Make the TO periods short, i.e., 2 to 5 minutes. It is better to have frequent, short TO's than a few very long ones. Be sure to give a TO every time a child cannot behave appropriately with others. Consistency in using TO is more important than severity. Make it swift and sure. Give it early enough to prevent misdeeds from escalating in severity.

4.   The TO period begins only after the child quiets down in the TO area. If the child carries on for five minutes in TO than he must remain for another five minutes while being quiet — for a total of ten minutes. Ignore any inquiries by the child about when TO is over. You might set a kitchen timer to be sure to remember when TO is up.

5. After TO is over redirect the child to appropriate behaviors and praise the child for being quiet in TO, and praise again when he or she begins behaving well.
6. TO works best with preschool and school age children rather than teenagers.

3. *Direct Application of Pain.* Apart from deprivation and restitution, you can penalize a child for misconduct by directly inflicting psychological or physical pain. You can impose psychological discomfort, for example, by stern disapprovals ("I don't like that!" "It makes me very angry when you do that!") and reprimands ("No! Don't do that!"). Verbal disapprovals and reprimands are probably the most frequent forms of punishment used in our society. Examples of physical pain include spanking, shaking, and squeezing. If one must spank a child, the "quick-lick" spanking seems best wherein you quickly spank hard enough to cause discomfort but not so severe as to be abusive. In using the above procedure, it is important to remember not to be insulting or demeaning to a child by name calling or sarcasm ("You dummy. . .how could you do such a thing?"), and blaming ("I don't understand how you could do such a thing! What an awful thing to do!").

Guidelines for Imposing Penalties

The following general guidelines are offered with a view of assisting you to think about and evaluate your effectiveness in imposing penalties on children.

1. *Be Explicit.* In order to avoid any possible misunderstanding by the child about why he is being punished, you should do three things: name the misbehavior; state the rule or principle that is being broken by the misdeed; and describe the punishment or unpleasant consequence that the child will receive because of the infraction. An example of a brief, explicit statement is: "John, you decided to go off grounds today, which is against the rules, so now you'll have to miss our next scheduled trip to Mohansic Park this Thursday."

By clearly and explicitly linking his misbehavior with the penalty, you weaken any efforts by the child to blame you for the punishment he has earned. Be sure to emphasize to the child that he had a choice in the situation and that by deciding to perform the deviant act, he elected to experience the adverse consequences. Your goal should be to promote self-criticism and confession in the child and to prevent him from avoiding responsibility by such tactics as denial (i.e., "I didn't do anything wrong."), rationalization (i.e., "Everybody is doing it."), or projection (i.e., "He started it.").

2. *Point out Acceptable Alternatives.* Punishment is designed to teach a child what not to do. A child will be more likely to change his inappropriate behavior, however, when he not only knows what he should not do, but what he should do. When punishing a child, then, take the time to explain what you consider to be acceptable behavior in that particular situation, e.g., "Joan, blocks are for building things, not for throwing around." Good discipline is a positive force that is oriented towards what a child is allowed to do, rather than what he is forbidden to do.

3. *Disapprove the Behavior, Not the Child.* The message you want to convey by using punishment is that, while you disapprove of certain of the child's actions, you still strongly approve of the child himself. Thus, you should avoid expressing global disapproval of the whole child, e.g., "I don't like you for that." or "You bad boy." Rather, your reaction should be limited to specific behaviors, e.g., "I don't like your loud screaming in the house."

The message you want to get across by enforcing a limit is that the child made a mistake in judgment for which he or she must accept responsibility. You want to avoid the message that the child is a bad or evil person who has terrible faults. Parents should expect children to make mistakes and then to suffer the consequences of these errors. Don't demand perfection from the children and become incensed when they do not live up to your unrealistic expectations. Try to avoid discouraging a child by taking his or her misconduct as a personal affront or terrible failure. Blaming, damning or threatening to withdraw love after a misdeed only compounds the problem by lowering the child's self-esteem.

4. *Be Consistent.* A common fault recognized by parents who have problems disciplining children is lack of consistency. Adults should strive for both inter- and intra-personal consistency in imposing penalties. Inter-personal consistency means that all the supervising adults in the home apply essentially the same penalties for a misdeed. Too often a strict father and a permissive mother will try to balance each other out by becoming stricter or more permissive in their punishment, as the case may be. This balancing approach tends to confuse children by confronting them with extremely divergent reactions and a "two wrongs make a right" approach. Husbands and wives must resolve differing philosophies of childrearing and personality conflicts if they want to avoid placing their children in the middle of a power struggle.

Intrapersonal consistency means your child can expect — over time — the same penalty from you for a specific misdeed. Don't set a penalty one day and a completely different type of consequence the next day — depending on your whims or emotional state. Intrapersonal consistency also means that you impose a penalty every time it is warranted, regardless of how tired you feel. If a child repeats the same infraction and you ignore it one day but impose a penalty the next, this uncertainty will undoubtedly result in an argument with the child to justify the punishment. The more confident you are in your authority and the more vigilant you are in applying penalties each time a particular misconduct occurs, the more your child will accept the penalties without protest and argument. Consistency, however, does not mean rigidity; rules can be bent a little in extraordinary occasions and emergencies. On the other hand, it does mean insisting on *action* from the child, not talk or promises that "I'll be good next time." or "Give me one more chance." The sooner children learn you mean what you say, that penalties are almost a certainty for specific offenses, the better for all concerned.

5. *Develop A Generally Supportive Relationship.* Children accept punishment best when they have a positive relationship with the adult, e.g., the adult tends to be generally warm, rewarding, accepting, and supportive of the child. If a child feels only

marginally accepted, your use of punishment will tend to solidify his negative view of you. Within a positive relationship, the most painful aspect of punishment for a child tends to be the disapproval or disappointment of the valued adult. In a good relationship, you will be most influential when a child has found it emotionally satisfying to want to be like you and to care about what you think of his behavior.

6. *Gather All The Facts.* Before punishing the child, you should calmly, deliberately, and objectively gather all the relevant facts. Moreover, if you adopt a causal approach and seek to determine why the child misbehaved, you will be in a better position to not only set a just penalty, but to eliminate the basic cause of the difficulty by understanding the child's motives. Be sure to allow the child to explain his side of the story. In this regard, mothers have been found to listen to children more than fathers, and thus tend to make better disciplinarians. When you find you have acted too hastily and made a mistake in punishing a child, admit your error immediately.

7. *Use Only As Last Resort.* Since punishment generally indicates failure to a child — and frequent failure experiences can lower self-esteem and confidence — it is best to concentrate more on positive reinforcement of socially acceptable behavior than on suppression of misbehavior by punishment. Of course, there will be times when penalties must be imposed, but positive methods should be used much more frequently so that you establish an approval-disapproval ratio of about 3 or 4 to 1. The social climate in a home seems to a large extent to be influenced by the approval-disapproval ratio employed by the parents. So make greater use of the more positive forms of discipline such as praise, rewards, modeling, reasoning, persuasion, and diversion.

8. *Timing.* Studies have shown that punishment is generally most effective in fostering learning when it immediately follows the misdeed. It is even more effective when it is applied as the child is in the act, i.e., as the child reaches for the materials from the supply cabinet, rather than after he already has them. Delay can cause a child to forget what he or she did to deserve the penalty.

The adult who experiences or first discovers the problem, should be the one to impose the penalty. In view of this, mothers should avoid saying, "Wait until your father gets home." The timing is not only poor when this is done, but this places the father in the role of villain who must assume an unfair share of rule enforcements.

9. *Reward Positive Behavior.* The carrot and stick approach is certainly more effective than the stick alone. So rather than punishing a child for a misdeed, try to strengthen by positive reinforcement (praise, rewards) alternate pro-social behaviors that will compete with the misdeed. For example, be sure to praise a child for sharing his possessions with his peers rather than just punishing him when he grabs his toys away from others. Too often adults take good behaviors for granted, assuming virtue is its own reward.

10. *Monitor Effects on Child.* Children's reactions to punishment are a very individual thing. Some kids have severe emotional reactions to certain forms of punishment. A very insecure, fearful child, for example, may become quite upset if isolated for a period of time in his room. Consider the child's feelings about the punishment since they are as important as the punishment itself. If a child is already feeling remorseful about the mistake, guilty scolding by you may lead to discouragement and depression. In this case, the child needs encouragement rather than criticism.

11. *Child Involvement.* Before externally imposing blame or guilt upon a child for his misdeed, allow him the opportunity to evaluate his own culpability in the situation. Thus, you might ask, "What did you do?" rather than encouraging the child to project all the blame onto others. After several dodges, the child will usually come up with at least a partial description of his involvement. Encourage your child to assess his behavior in terms of its helpfulness to others and to himself. ("Did your actions help others? Help yourself?")

Occasionally, try allowing children to determine their own punishment. This will encourage kids to be more reflective and responsible for their own actions. If a child gives himself an excessive punishment, you can always tone it down. If the punishment is too light, try it once and see if it proves to be effective.

12. *Be Calm and Matter-of-Fact.* Explain a punishment to a child in a calm and matter-of-fact manner, much like a salesman announcing the price of something or a judge reading a decision. Avoid name-calling, yelling, insults, sarcasm and other judgmental, critical techniques which only lower a child's self-esteem while increasing his emotional reaction. A punishment should highlight conflict between a child's behavior and a very sensible rule or principle, while minimizing any personal conflict between you and the child. Remember that children pay more attention to the nonverbal communications of the punishing adult than to the verbal ones. If you discipline with an enraged look, a vocal tone five times higher than usual, and hands trembling, they will feel unloved and disliked, no matter what you say verbally. When you punish out of hostility the child will sense this and see it as vengence rather than justice. So administer punishments as matter-of-factly as possible. When you stay calm and confident, the child will get over his anger much quicker. The means you use to punish are probably secondary to your emotional attitude in giving the penalty. Children will learn you are every bit as serious when speaking calmly as when screaming. Moreover, research has shown that the more emotional you are in punishing, the more severe will be the punishment you impose. Your attitude should be that of a teacher, i.e., wanting to help the child learn.

One way to stay calm is to expect kids to rebel against your authority as part of the normal process of growing up and developing their own identity. We should expect some nonconformity at times, then, and not overreact by taking it personally. On those occasions when you simply cannot keep in your anger or annoyance, simply tell the child exactly how angry you are at the misbehavior. In other words, express your anger by focusing on your feelings and needs rather than trying to hurt the child by insults, threats, or other demeaning comments.

13. *Be Just.* In the interest of justice, be sure to consider the following in imposing a penalty: first or repeated offense; premeditated or impulsive act, general character and conduct, and any extenuating circumstances.

14. *No Double Jeopardy.* Be sure that the child is not punished by two different sources for the same offense, e.g., both teacher and parent punish child for the same behavior.

15. *Privacy.* A cardinal rule in discipline is that almost without exception, warnings and penalties should be administered to a child as privately as possible. No one likes to be criticized in public and we react with open or hidden resentment when this happens. In accord with the golden rule, we should treat children as we would like to be treated.

16. *Try For Prevention.* If you carefully analyze situations in which discipline breaks down, you may discover certain patterns. You may find, for example, that your preschool child becomes extremely irritable in the late morning when he misses his naps. Just before dinner time has been found to be a troublesome time for school-age children because they are hungry and tired at this time. Knowledge of these patterns should help you prevent them next time, e.g., provide more snacks, naps or quiet times. Also, consider the time and type of day (rainy weather), previous activities of the child, and what new activities were beginning (if during a transitional period, you might want to provide more supervision or structure.

17. *Combine With Support.* After being punished, a child particularly needs your immediate warmth and understanding. This will not negate the lesson, but will keep your child from feeling unloved. Young children especially have a tendency to feel rejected and unloved when punished by their parents. By being friendly and warm to a child after disciplining him you demonstrate that it was the misdeed you disapproved of, not the child. Introduce a positive note as soon as possible by praising the child for taking the penalty well; then redirect the child's attention to alternate acceptable behaviors. The period after a child has completed a penalty is often a good time to have a heart-to-heart talk about the problem. By being friendly and supportive after imposing a penalty, you can break the negative emotional climate aroused by the punishment.

18. *Vicarious Experience.* Research has indicated that, if children learn that their peers or siblings have been punished for misdeeds, they are less likely to engage in the particular misbehaviors

themselves for a time. Thus, children in a large group home can learn a great deal about appropriate behavior just be keeping their eyes and ears open. You can also assist them in gaining vicarious experience by reading stories or articles about deviant youths who have experienced adverse consequences of their antisocial actions.

19. *Give a Warning.*   Before imposing a penalty, warn the child once that it's imminent; if the child has received repeated warnings in the past, then you can dispense with this advance notice.

20. *Avoid Perfectionistic Tendencies.*   Helping children become mature, self-disciplined individuals requires mature, self-disciplined adults. However, no parent can be ideal nor should one expect to be perfect. We all have our angry, impatient, and unfair moments in imposing penalties. These occasional emotional reactions will not impair our relationship with the child.

Of course, we should try to improve our self-control and disciplinary techniques without imposing unrealistically high standards upon ourselves. Raising children gives us a unique opportunity to know ourselves better and to grow in maturity. As Thoreau once said, "There is a child in every parent who needs to learn discipline."

Epilogue

The final goal of imposing penalties is to teach children to develop their own inner controls. The children's reactions to their misdeeds will give you valuable insights into your effectiveness as a disciplinarian. Consider how they typically react when they have misbehaved and caused harm to others. If they usually react with guilt, confession, and constructive efforts to undo the harm, then you know you are on the right track in that they have internalized parental interdictions and formed a conscience. On the other hand, if they tend to react with denials, Watergate-type coverups, projection of blame onto others, avoidance of adults who punish, or with attempts to rationalize away all personal responsibility, then you should probably consider reviewing and/or changing your disciplinary practices. Children who persist in engaging in antisocial acts because of underlying psychological problems or value differences will probably need therapy, not repeated punishment by parents.

DECIDING WHEN AND HOW OFTEN TO GIVE SANCTIONS

When to Give

A well-established learning principle is that the sooner young children receive a sanction (reward or penalty) following their behavior, the more effective these sanctions or reinforcers will be in changing the frequency with which the behaviors occur. In other words, the longer the delay between the child's behavior and the parent's response, the less effective the learning will be. Thus, young children should receive immediate feedback from their parents in the form of positive or negative reinforcements.

For example, a parent who gives his child a penalty immediately following a misdeed, or better yet during the execution of the misdeed will be more effective in decreasing the frequency of this misdeed than a parent who says, "I'll talk to you about that later." or "Wait until your daddy gets home!" So if you look out your kitchen window and discover your preschool child is picking flowers from your garden but you are tied up and can't say anything to the child right away, don't try to punish the child several hours later. Rather, it would be better to wait until the child repeats the act and then administer a warning or penalty. You want the child to associate unpleasant consequences with flower picking, not something the child is doing several hours later.

Also, rather than telling a teenager that "You can't go to the party next week.", give a more immediate penalty like loss of TV or telephone privileges. Nobody likes to have something hanging over their head for a week.

If you must delay giving an immediate reward or penalty to young child, give a symbol or token immediately to indicate that the sanction will be conferred.

Discussion

As a child matures, he will be more able to anticipate future reinforcers and will have less of a need for immediate consequences. Still, you will often find that children will be unable to persevere at long, difficult tasks. Children often drop music lessons, for example, because practicing is hard work and the joys of playing are minimal in the early stages. The solution to this difficulty may lie in finding a more immediate incentive for the child, such as learning to play in school with one's close friends, or learning to play with the immediate goal of qualifying for the school band.

One of the main advantages of taking short steps in route to a major objective is that success with the initial efforts tends to fuel and sustain longer term efforts. It is very difficult for a teenager to sustain his effort in studying physics or chemistry solely on the basis of his goal of becoming a doctor some day. He needs a more immediate payoff, such as good grades or otherwise taking each course as a challenging task in itself.

How Often to Give

Kids learn slowly and forget quickly. To be effective in changing a child's behavior, you will have to reinforce their behavior more than once. Be patient and repeat the reinforcers on different occasions. In general, children do not learn things once and for all. Slow learners and/or emotionally disturbed children, in particular, will require a large number of learning trials.

Research has shown that children learn a new behavior faster if they are reinforced every time they perform the behavior. However, if you constantly reinforce children after they have learned an act, then they will not maintain it as well as if you reinforce them occasionally. So it seems best for you to reinforce a child 100 percent of the time until he has mastered the behavior, and then give him only occasional reinforcement, e.g., once for every two or three occurrences of the behavior, to be sure the behavior is continued over time. The fact that an occasional reward is all that is needed to keep one at something indefinitely has been called the "Las Vegas" principle, since the behavior of the slot machine faithfuls and other gamblers attests to the power of this motivation.

USING PHYSICAL CONTROL

Physical coercion or force should generally be the last control method to be used. It should be employed only when all the other techniques of influencing children have failed. Being responsible for children, however, means that you sometimes cannot be tolerant of a child's lack of compliance or cooperation. Legitimate coercion consists of either taking children by the arm and preventing them from engaging in some harmful action; leading or carrying them in a desired direction, e.g., to another room; or restraining them from continuing a dangerous behavior.

When using physical coercion, you should remain calm but firm. Show determination, but not hostility. Avoid yelling or glaring at the child. In a matter-of-fact manner explain the reason you are using physical force, i.e., how he brought it on himself by deciding to continue to act inappropriately even though you had warned him of the consequences.

At times your child may have a temper tantrum so severe that he will have to be restrained so as to protect either himself, others, or property. A particularly effective procedure for restraining an out-of-control child is to stand behind him and securely place your arms around his. When you stand behind a child, you lessen the danger of your being kicked by him. While holding an upset child, you should continually express calm, reassuring words, such as "It's going to be all right."; "Just relax."; "I won't let any harm come to you."; "As soon as you have calmed down, I'll let you go." In a time of crisis such as this, a child with poor impulse control needs to feel that he can draw upon the strength of an adult. Holding or restraining a child should be done in a firm but nonpainful way. Use only as much force as is actually needed to control the child. Physical restraint and coercion are not intended to be forms of physical punishment!

Discussion

Physical control should not be confused with corporal punishment, which involves the infliction of physical pain on a child by such practices as spanking, striking, shaking, pinching, or forcing a child to stand or kneel for long periods of time. Although there is still considerable controversy among experts about spanking kids, there seem to be more humane ways of punishing a child than the use of physical pain.

Section B
Child Guidance Skills

CREATIVE PROBLEM-SOLVING

Social adjustment can be viewed as a continuous process of meeting new problematic situations and finding ways of coping with them. Developing a creative problem-solving procedure is an effective way to cope with the problems of living. Children need to develop the attitude that it is in their best interest to recognize and face up to personal problems, that problems are an inevitable part of living, and that most of them can be solved. This positive orientation will tend to counter tendencies in children to look toward parents to solve all of their difficulties or to be afraid of working on a solution for fear of being proven wrong or inept. With the proper training, they will learn to avoid the common tendencies of either impulsively attacking a problem without thinking it through or delaying doing anything about a problem in the hope that it will go away.

Research has now established that parents can teach children each of the five steps in the problem solving process: 1) Identifying a problem and specifying a workable goal for resolving it. 2) Generating alternate solutions to meet the goal. 3) Evaluating and deciding on the best solution. 4) Implementing the solution. 5) Follow-up evaluations to see if the plan is working. Studies have also shown that the second step in the problem solving process, generating alternate solutions, is a particularly important skill to teach preschool children since it is related to social adjustment in children this age. Adolescents, on the other hand, seem to profit most from guidance in how to implement a possible solution to a problem, i.e., the fourth step in effective problem solving.

In another section of the book, the first step in solving personal problems is discussed, i.e., helping children select specific, manageable goals to begin working on. This section will focus on the ability to generate many different solutions to a problem.

Teaching Children to Think of Alternate Solutions

The second step in the creative problem-solving process is the ability to think up as many solutions to a problem as possible. This is a valuable skill for your child to develop since there is usually more than one way to solve a problem and some solutions will be better than others. Like other thinking skills, it improves and becomes more efficient with practice.

You can develop this skill by posing hypothetical situations to your child, such as "What would you do if a child, much younger than yourself, started hitting you?" Then encourage the child to think of as many possible solutions to the problem as possible while you write them down. Rather than just variations on a theme, seek different categories or types of solutions. For example, your child might suggest the following:

"Hit him back."
"Just walk away."
"Tell him to stop it."
"Tell his mother."
"Tell him it hurt and I didn't like it."; or
"Ask a teacher to talk to him."

Pose other hypothetical problems like, "Suppose a boy has been playing with a toy for a long time, say all morning, and now his brother wants to play with it. In what ways can this problem be solved?" Or, you might say, "Suppose a girl just broke her mommy's glasses by accident. What could she do or say so her mommy won't be mad?" If your child is unable to think of many solutions, you could help by suggesting other possibilities.

After the initial development of this skill via hypothetical situations (which tend to be nonanxiety provoking), try asking your children to come up with alternate solutions to a real life problem they are experiencing.

Be sure to make these problem solving periods fun and exciting for you and your child. Avoid criticizing or ridiculing any of the children's solutions — no matter how silly or far-fetched they may seem. Rather, encourage your child to think of imaginative and "far out" ideas. Try to be a good model by giving imaginative, creative solutions yourself. Be sure to praise a child for facing a real problem and trying to solve it. Also, express your appreciation for the child's thoughts, e.g., "That was a good idea."

After generating possible solutions, the next step in the problem solving process is for the child to make a decision as to the best solution. Critical evaluation is involved here which means weighing the possible consequences (pros and cons) of each solution. Once the best solution has been selected, the next step is to carefully come up with step-by-step plans for implementing the solution. Roles must be defined (who does what and when) and forethought is needed to avoid possible pitfalls. After the means for achieving the goal have been specified, the final step is to help the child to observe how well the plan works and to make revisions or go to alternate plans as needed.

When children learn to independently form hypotheses as to the best way to solve problems and then proceed to systematically test and evaluate their hypotheses, they are practicing the scientific or empirical method of problem-solving. This thoughtful rather than impulsive method of resolving difficulties is an important aspect of character development.

In addition to offering problem-solving training, you should be a model of effective problem-solving attitudes and approaches. When difficulties arise, children who hear "Let's see what we can do." more often than "It's just no use! I don't know what we're going to do!" learn that problems can be tackled effectively. What is needed is a combination of a "can do" spirit and creative problem-solving skills. Also, wishful thinking tends to be characteristic of children (I wish a good fairy would bring me riches) versus a problem-solving approach (I'll go out and get a part-time job). From an early age, then, children need to cultivate a constructive problem-solving attitude rather than a magical approach to life's problems.

ADDITIONAL READING

Spivack, G., Platt, J.J., and Shure, M.B. *The Problem-Solving Approach to Adjustment.* Jossey-Bass Publishers, 1976.

REASONING

Reasoning refers to the ability to think logically and form judgments, as well as to the ability to draw inferences and conclusions from the given facts. Once children have reached the elementary school years, you should be sure to give them explanations or reasons for behaving in certain ways rather than expecting blind obedience. For example, you might say to a child: "Jim, you could get hurt doing that." or "It's important to learn arithmetic because you need it for a lot of jobs you might want to get when you grow up." or "It's important to learn arithmetic so that people will think you are smart and not dumb." By doing so you would be teaching your children to anticipate immediate and long-term consequences of their actions and to see that there is usually a cause-and-effect ("if-then") relationship between what we do and what later happens to us. If I do this, then this will happen to me.

By helping children anticipate the various consequences of their actions, you will be aiding them to develop a future time perspective whereby they can imagine or foresee the personal rewards or penalties that will be forthcoming as a result of their actions. Once children develop this ability, they will be better able to control their tendency toward seeking immediate gratification of impulses.

In addition to anticipating the personal consequences of a course of action, help your children foresee the consequences of their actions on other people: "If I do this, then it will probably have this effect on others." Empathy or the ability to put yourself in someone else's shoes is an extremely important aspect of socialization. It is discussed in more detail in another section of this book.

When parents initially set or enforce a rule with a child they should explain the reason, i.e., the adverse effect on self or others if the rule is broken. State the reason in a clear and concise way. Do not give a long lecture or sermon which will tend to turn the child off. Also, state the reason only once or twice, and do not let the child draw you into a long debate or argument about it. Often when you give an explanation about a rule, the child will try to turn this into an argument by quizzing you, rebutting your reasons, or pointing out exceptions to the rule. Avoid this trap by briefly stating the reason and then cutting off debate by insisting upon compliance to the rule. In other words, exert your authority and do not feel as though children have to always accept the logic of your reasons. Indeed, you do not have to attempt to justify *all* your directions. At times you should feel free to say, "Do it because I say so!"

Inductive and Deductive Reasoning

Apart from promoting the ability to anticipate the consequences of one's acts, you will want to stimulate your children to think inductively and deductively. Inductive reasoning refers to the ability to draw general principles or conclusions from specific things that have happened to us or to others. To encourage this form of abstract thinking, you might observe how certain truths seem to hold up across different situations, times, and people: "Joan, have you noticed that whenever one of your classmates doesn't want to play by the rules of a game, nobody wants to be their friend anymore?" Or you might say: "It seems to me that whenever one of your friends is with Louise a lot, that friend gets into trouble. I wonder if that could be true?" Another way to encourage inductive reasoning is to get into the habit of asking your children what the moral is of a story, movie, or TV show.

Deductive reasoning refers to the ability to use general principles or rules to govern one's specific behaviors. One such general principle that would be helpful for a child to learn early is the golden rule, do unto others as you would have them do unto you. Another useful principle for children to apply to their daily lives is that if you want others to like you, you should act friendly, helpful and cooperative towards them. Also, teaching children to use proverbs, maxims, and adages in governing their behavior is an excellent way to stimulate deductive thinking.

In conclusion, it is noteworthy that research studies have suggested that the more you use reasoning with your children and encourage them to use it, the higher will be the children's level of moral development.

OFFERING ADVICE

Advice is like snow; the softer it falls, the longer it dwells upon, and the deeper it sinks into the mind.

Coleridge

To advise a child means to offer tentative suggestions for solving a problem based on your expertise (knowledge, experience, common sense) or objective perspective. Giving advice is particularly appropriate when a child is a rank beginner and you have expert or relevant knowledge to share. Advice is best received when it is in response to a child's request for it. However, most children are reluctant to ask questions about certain topics (sex, drugs) so that you should offer to frankly discuss such taboo topics, or simply raise the question yourself and proceed to talk about it.

To be effective in giving advice or counsel, you have to establish yourself as an expert on the subject in the eyes of the child, i.e., a person with superior knowledge and/or experience. This means functioning as an authoritative parent, that is, a parent who does not make statements or predictions unless he or she is well informed about a topic. So well informed, in fact, that one can readily substantiate personal statements with reference material. Before offering advice about such topics as sex, drugs, or smoking, you should read up on all the available information relating to these topics. Federal and state governments offer many excellent pamphlets and books on these subjects, both for parents and for children.

Be sure that you are prepared to offer advice early in a child's development. It has been found, for instance, that it is best to provide children with antismoking information at about the fifth grade level. This is the age when most youngsters begin to experiment with cigarettes.

In giving advice, you attempt to share with a child information or experiences that you believe will be valuable. You usually only give advice once and then you *leave the decision to the child.* It is different from preaching wherein you proclaim, often in a tiresome manner, a given course of action as the one and only course to follow. In other words, when you preach, you strongly and persistently urge your child to conform to your recommendations.

Pitfalls in Offering Advice

1. *Manner in Which Given.* The manner in which you give advice may be more important than the content. Avoid being a "Father knows best" know-it-all who makes authoritarian pronouncements, or being a "Helpful Henry" who is constantly bombarding others with offhand suggestions on how to run their lives. Also avoid trying to live your life over again through

your children so that you project your own needs, desires, and goals into the child's situation. Rather, offer advice in a tentative manner so that the child feels free to accept or reject it. Thus, rather than saying, "You certainly must listen to this. . .", say, "Some people have tried this." or "You might want to consider this approach to your problem."

2. *Positive Relationship.* Advice is most effective when your relationship with the child is characterized by mutual trust and respect.

3. *Expect Noncompliance.* In offering advice, you have to be willing to accept the fact that children will generally not follow it. Moreover, if they happen to take your advice and find it invalid they may blame you.

4. *Draw the Child Out.* Sometimes when children seek advice they know fully well what to do. Rather than promote a dependency relationship, hand the responsibility back to the child ("I think you'll be able to figure this one out by yourself."), or simply reflect the child's dependency feeling ("Sounds like you lost confidence in your own judgment.").

On other occasions, children will have the answer within themselves and it only needs to be drawn out. The best procedure here is to give indirect advice by using the Socratic method of *directive questioning* to elicit the solution from the child. By skillful use of questions, you can help a child focus on the relevant aspects of the problem or apply knowledge already possessed that is related to the problem at hand. For example, some questions you might use when a child is afraid of a neighborhood bully are: "Do you think you are strong enough to fight him yourself?"; "How do little birds handle a big bird that is bothering them?"; "What do you think the bully is afraid of?"; or "How do the other kids handle the bully problem?"

5. *Use Sparingly.* Give advice sparingly because even when handled well, it has a tendency to make a child feel dumb, inferior, or overly controlled.

Proverbial Sayings

A quick and simple way to give advice is to use a relevant maxim or proverb. A proverb is a short, concise saying in common use that strikingly expresses an age-old truth, rule of conduct, or familiar experience. Examples of common sayings are:

"If there's a will there's a way."

"If it's worth doing at all, it's worth doing well."

"Easy come, easy go."

"A stitch in time saves nine."

Because common sayings seem so trite, most of us can hardly bring ourselves to say them. Nevertheless, they embody the concentrated experience and wisdom of the human race. If a child was to regulate his life according to their general truths, he would not go far wrong. Ordinary common sense, then, provides an extensive and highly valid understanding of human nature. For this reason, common sayings deserve more attention than they have received of late. They are also an excellent way to teach a child to use deductive reasoning, i.e., application of general principles to guide one's life. Their judicious use in childrearing can inspire, explain, and provide comfort to children.

In offering a maxim to a child, you should clearly state that it is not an original idea of yours. Rather, introduce the adage by saying, "It's been said. . ." or "They say. . ." or "There's an old saying that I like which you might find helpful in your present situation." The more you have found an adage to be helpful in your personal life, the more persuasive you will be in presenting the advice to a child.

Parents who find it difficult to use the more common maxims might feel more comfortable offering little known but equally meaningful quotes, such as:

> There is nothing so easy but that it becomes difficult when you do it with reluctance.
>
> Terrence Timoroumenos

> If you are searching for truth, just stop cherishing opinions.
>
> Sixth Patriarch of Zen
> (700 years ago)

The following adages point to the positive value of platitudes:

> We frequently fall into error and folly, not because the true principles of action are not known, but because for a time they are not remembered; he may, therefore, justly be numbered among the

benefactors of mankind who contracts the great rules of life into short sentences that may early be impressed on the memory, and taught by frequent recollection to occur habitually to the mind.

Johnson

The proverbial wisdom of the populace in the street, on the roads, and in the markets, instructs the ear of him who studies man more fully than a thousand rules ostentatiously displayed.

Lavater

Story-Telling

Since every child responds to and enjoys story-telling, you can help your children solve their problems by indirectly giving advice via a story. For instance, you might tell a story about your own childhood which pertains to the child's present problem, e.g., "When I was about your age, I had a similar problem with a bully. Do you want to know what happened?" Since children identify so readily with animals, you might also tell a fable, i.e., a story depicting how animals solved a similar problem. You could relate, for instance, how birds solve a difficulty involving bigger birds (or humans) bullying on them. They typically get a large group together and harass the bigger bird by hit and run tactics.

Thus, by telling stories or parables that contain healthy adaptations to problems, you aid children to perceive events in a new light and to generate new solutions to difficulties. Such allegorical communications are generally received with less anxiety than messages presented in undisguised form.

In relating stories, cultivate the art of the story-teller, i.e., surprise twists in the story, use gestures, vary your tone of voice, show interest and wonder yourself, use dialogue and humor, and involve the child by stopping to ask questions: "And what do you think happened next?".

Reflective Stories. This technique is for use with preschoolers when you suspect them of a misdeed but you are not certain and need to obtain more information. Try telling them a story about children of the same age, sex, appearance, home environment, and situation. For example, a father seeking to determine why his toddlers are fighting could tell the following story to the older child:

Joan, you're such a pretty four-year-old girl — with a younger brother. I'm going to tell you a story. Once upon a time, a long, long time ago, across the mountains and over the seas there lived a girl named Maryanne. She had pretty blue eyes and was also four years old. She had a little brother like you. One day Maryanne was playing with her little brother when her mother heard the little brother crying. Why do you think Maryanne's little brother was crying?   Joan: Because he took Maryanne's toy, and she hit him.

This procedure works remarkably well with young children because they do not have the power to think abstractly. It is extremely difficult for most parents, however, to believe that their children will not see through this procedure.

ADDITIONAL READING

The following are inexpensive reference books that will enable you to offer well-informed advice on sex and drugs:

1. *What To Tell Children About Sex.* (Prepared by The Child-Study Association.) Pocket Books Edition, New York, 1974.
2. Chauney, H.W. and Kirkpatrick, L.A. *Drugs and You.* Oxford Book Co., New York, 1970. (It contains a discussion of tobacco and alcohol.)
3. *You, Your Child, and Drugs.* (Prepared by The Child-Study Association of America.) Child Study Press, New York, 1971.

An excellent description of the reflective stories technique is contained in:

Madsen, C.K. and Madsen, C.H. Jr. Parents-Children-Discipline: A Positive Approach. Allyn and Bacon, Boston, p. 157, 1972.

UNDERSTANDING WHY CHILDREN MISBEHAVE

There are two basic approaches to enforcing limits with children: the surface approach focuses primarily on controlling the observable behavior of children; the causal approach seeks not only to control or regulate behavior, but to understand the basic causes of the child's misbehavior. The causal approach looks for the underlying motives and intentions of an act and seeks to ferret out *why* a child acted as he did. By way of analogy, rather than controlling a dandelion by picking off the top — only to have it regrow in a week — a causal approach would be to try to solve the problem by eliminating the hidden root.

Epitomizing the surface approach would be an "Archie Bunker" type of parent, i.e., one who is rigid, authoritarian, and who expects blind obedience from children. Following this approach one would apply the letter rather than the spirit of the law. This type of person judges the seriousness of an act in accord with its practical consequences, e.g., an accidental spilling of a pitcher of milk would be considered a more serious offense than the intentional spilling of a cupful of milk. Such a parent would not be inclined to take into account the circumstances in which a misdeed occurred or the hidden motives of the child. Moreover, this parent is more inclined to apply moral labels to children, e.g., "John's a bad, mean child.", and then respond to the label rather than to the child and the specific situation.

The causal approach, on the other hand, assumes that every behavior of a child is motivated, i.e., the child perceives a good reason or purpose for it. Usually these causes are not apparent at the conscious level. The child does not know why he does the things he does, so there is no sense in asking him why he did it. Yet parents must try to ascertain and understand the child's motives. Among the more common motives for troublesome behavior in children are:

1. *Attention.* Children want so much for their parents to notice them that they would rather get negative attention (verbal admonishments and criticism) from them than get no attention at all.

2. *Vengeance.* A child who feels hurt or frustrated by you may try to get even or save face by being rebellious or defiant towards you at some later date.

3. *Misappraisals.* A child may simply misunderstand what was expected of him or forget the rules.

4. *Power Struggle.* Children often act in troublesome ways to convince you to give in and let them have their way in a dispute.

5. *Physical Cause.* The child is feeling irritable because he or she is tired, hungry, or sick.

6. *Sibling Rivalry.* The child is jealous of attention or favors granted to a sibling or peer.
7. *Displacement.* The child has suffered some blow to self-esteem and seeks to take it out on you.
8. *Values.* The child acts in an egocentric way and shows little concern for others or guilt over a transgression.

Techniques of the Causal Approach

Among the procedures you could employ to discover and verify the underlying causes of a child's misbehavior are the following:

1. *Observation.* Carefully observe the child's typical behavior patterns, e.g., does he misbehave with certain people and not with others?; does he act up at certain times of the day only?; does the child show any physical symptoms of illness?
2. *Listen.* Listen carefully to the child's side of the story. Ask him to explain the events and details leading up to the misdeed. Focus on the thoughts and feelings which prompted the act. Show respect and interest in what he has to say about the situation.
3. *Be Empathetic.* Put yourself in the child's shoes and try to see the situation from his perspective. Consider what he must have thought and felt before, during, and after the misbehavior. Carefully analyze whether you have been overlooking some of his basic needs, e.g., love, attention, competence, acceptance, understanding.
4. *Consultation.* Consult with others who know the child well, e.g., teachers, siblings, peers, as to their opinion about why the child is misbehaving.

After you have formed a reasonable hypothesis as to the possible reasons for the child's misdeeds, test out the accuracy of these hypotheses by such techniques as:

1. *Interpretation.* Conjecture to your child the reason you consider to be the main cause of his misdeeds, e.g., "I wonder if you're missing Mommy when she goes to work, so you feel kinda mean and don't want to obey the babysitter?"
2. *Experiment.* Take an experimental, problem-solving approach to discover the root cause. For example, if you suspect that

your child is misbehaving because of a felt lack of parental attention, try offering the child more of your individual attention and see if this results in a perceptible improvement in the child's behavior. If no change is apparent after a reasonable period, try testing out an alternate hypothesis. The experimental approach takes a lot of patience, analysis, and careful observation to be effective, but it is often the only way to really discover what is bothering your child.

INTERPRETING POSSIBLE REASONS FOR MISBEHAVIOR

Asking children why they misbehave is generally fruitless because most children are not consciously aware of why they act as they do.

However, parents can often form a plausible explanation of why a child is misbehaving if they will look beyond the surface behavior for the underlying cause. One should try to infer what the child is trying to express by this behavior. What legitimate needs, if any, are not being satisfied. Try putting yourself in his or her shoes and seeing things from the perspective of the child's needs and motives.

The psychologist Abraham Maslow has stated that there are five basic needs that are important in everyone's lives:

1. physical, i.e., need for food, clothing, shelter, and rest;
2. safety, i.e., the need to be safe from harm or danger;
3. love, i.e., the need to feel that you belong and are loved;
4. self-worth, i.e., the need to feel competent and a person of worth, and
5. self-fulfillment, i.e., the need to develop all of one's potentialities.

Interference with any of these basic needs can lead to problem behavior. Among the other motives for misbehavior in a child are: attention-seeking; immediate gratification of impulses; desire to boss or dominate others; revenge for previous wrongs; and discouragement or poor self-esteem.

When your children fall into the habit of misbehaving, observe them carefully for an extended period. Under what circumstances (persons, times, places) do they usually become upset? If your son acts up when you praise or give attention to another sibling, then you might suspect that his need for attention and approval is unfulfilled.

You would then check the accuracy of this appraisal by making a conjecture to your child rather than giving a direct conclusion. For example, you might say, "I wonder if you get upset like this because you feel bad when Mommy and Daddy don't pay enough attention to you?" or "Could it be that you feel bad because you think we like Suzy better than you?"

To further illustrate, if a child has been trying to maintain an over-cheerful attitude after her father's death, the mother might suggest: "Mary, I wonder if thinking about your father is so painful that you just avoid all thoughts and feelings of him and his death?" Or if it is clear that your son has no friends because he is too bossy and bullies others (but the child does not recognize it), you might try to point this out by saying, "John, could it be that the reason the other kids don't play with you much is because when they don't do as you tell them, you throw sand at them and make them cry?" Or you might say to another child, "Jim, do you think Bruce hit you because you wouldn't share your toy?" Note that in the above examples, your interpretations are designed to focus the child's attention on his or her role in causing the problem. This is the kind of insight that can help children find effective solutions by themselves.

If you are on the wrong track with an interpretation (hypothesis as to possible cause), you just won't get a reaction. But if you have uncovered the real motive behind a child's misbehavior, you should immediately get a characteristic "recognition reaction" in the child, i.e., a roguish smile and a peculiar twinkle of the eyes, much like the cat who swallowed the canary.

An understanding of one's psychological needs and motives can lead to an immediate improvement in the problem behavior, especially in a young child.

Guidelines for Interpretations

1. *Manner.* Don't come on like a "know-it-all," seeking to dominate the child by your superior wisdom. Avoid communicating to the child the message: "You may think you know why you do certain things, but I know better." Rather be calm, friendly,

and tentative. Always give the interpretation in the form of a conjecture (Could it be. . . I wonder if. . . .) rather than a direct statement. If you come on as critical or fault-finding, the child is bound to feel defensive.

2. *Timing.* Never give an interpretation immediately after a misdeed, when both you and the child are upset. Select a quiet, relaxed time when you feel close to the child, e.g., just before bedtime. Also, be sensitive to a child's ability to handle an insight. Like a good gardener, wait until you recognize something that is struggling to emerge and then make it easier to surface. Finally, don't be in a hurry to interpret the first time a child misbehaves. You'll have plenty of chances to give an insight.

3. *Common Sense.* Avoid interpretations which require special expertise such as depth psychoanalysis, or insights based on theoretical frameworks such as transactional analysis. Rather limit yourself to matter-of-fact explanations which are employed in everyday life, that is, common sense observations. Common sense interpretations are a feature of everyday conversation between peoples in all walks of life. Stick to trying to understand the child's present actions, attitudes, and immediate purposes. Suggest what you believe the child wants to gain from the misbehavior.

4. *Know Your Child.* The more you know about your child's value system, motives, past experiences, personality traits, weaknesses, and strengths, the better your interpretations will be. You will also be more effective when you possess wide knowledge about human motivation in general.

5. *Listen With the Third Ear.* A skilled interpreter of human behavior has the ability to listen to the message behind words and to read between the lines of a letter. Become skilled in picking up nonverbal cues and in guessing the underlying psychological meaning of behavior. Like a good detective, you have to develop your powers of accurate observation and inference making. Parents readily do this with the nonverbal messages of infants, but they tend to become more judging and less understanding of the behavior of older children.

6. *Short and Simple.* Confine your interpretation to one sentence with young children, e.g., "I guess you're afraid you'll make a

mistake." or "Oh, maybe you're mad at your father?" Also, use simple, concrete language rather than abstract terms or jargon.

7. *Limited Goal.* Don't strive to give the final, complete, once-and-for-all insight that will miraculously change the child. Just strive to increase the child's self-knowledge a little by focusing on one possible motive for the misdeed.

8. *Sparingly.* Offer interpretations infrequently lest the children feel they are constantly being analyzed or that "big brother" is always observing them.

9. *Open Mind.* Keep an open mind about the possible reasons for a child's misbehavior. Avoid rigid, preconceived notions as to why your child exhibits problems.

10. *Seek Verification.* Validity is a problem when it comes to un-covering unconscious motivations. Only the child can really judge the accuracy of your insight, so be sure to seek verifica-tion from the child. The acid test of the usefulness of your interpretation is not only that the child accepts it as truthful, but that the child then acts upon this new insight in a positive way.

Discussion

By giving interpretations, you are modeling one form of reasoning, namely cause-and-effect thinking. Causal reasoning can be defined as the ability to relate one event to another over time with regard to the why that might have precipitated the act. Your ultimate goal in giv-ing interpretations is to stimulate children's ability to do their own causal thinking about their motives.

Apart from verbal speculations, you might offer interpretations in the form of metaphors or stories which may give the child a new in-sight into current behavior. Of course, the child should feel free to accept or reject these explanations. Leave it to the child to find some similarity in motives between the story characters and himself. To illustrate the use of metaphors, you might say, "Most of the time I see you as a great big stuffed animal that stays in any position placed." Or you might tell a story as follows: "I had a daydream about what you said yesterday. I imagined you were in a sailboat without a rudder and you were being blown about the ocean by the prevailing winds. Finally, you were blown into a strange port and you nonchalantly got out and walked towards the town whistling a happy tune. Does this seem like you?"

ADDITIONAL READING

Dreikurs, R. *The Challenge of Child Training.* Hawthorne Books, 1972. Contains a description of the use of parent interpretation with children.

DESENSITIZING FEARS

Trying to talk a child out of a fear is useless. So to help your children overcome an atypical fear of a particular object or event, try desensitizing them by gradually increasing their exposure to the feared object while they are otherwise comfortable and secure.

Often a *gradual* exposure to a feared object or situation is all that needs to be done. If a child is afraid of dogs, many parents overcome this by buying the child a cute, helpless puppy. In this way, as the puppy grows, the child gradually gets used to being around a bigger pet. Other parents attempt more systematic approaches. If a girl is afraid of dogs, for example, a parent might first read picture books about dogs, buy a toy dog, tell stories about the child and a funny dog having good times together, model dogs in clay, and then buy the child a puppy.

If your daughter is afraid of the dentist, you might have her wait outside his office while you go in for a minute to talk. Then the dentist might come outside to greet the child. Next the child might remain in the waiting room while you go for an appointment. The dentist would be sure to welcome the girl and give her candy or a treat. He would invite her to see his equipment and explain his work. Next the mother might arrange for the girl to accompany a fearless friend to the dentist's office while the friend has work done. Then the child would go for an appointment while the mother stayed nearby.

If your son is afraid of the dark, you might try to overcome this fear by the following steps:

1. Buy him an alarm clock with a luminescent face.
2. Watch TV with him in the dark.
3. Eat dinner with him by very faint candlelight.
4. Play games like hide and seek with him in the dark.
5. Sit with him in the dark and discuss pleasant topics.
6. Put a rheostat on the light in his room and slowly make it dimmer until the room is completely dark.

Each step up the ladder of overcoming a fear should be a little more difficult than the previous step, and you should only proceed to a higher step when you are certain the child experiences no fear with the current step. As you progress through the desensitization process, you may have to return to an earlier step if your child shows considerable fear or anxiety at a particular stage. This is a sign that you have moved too quickly. It should be noted that an especially strong fear of long standing will require a greater number of steps and a longer period to overcome. Sometimes, it takes six months to a year to overcome a deeply entrenched fear.

Discussion

To be sure your child is relaxed while you gradually present fear-arousing situations, you might have to provide pleasurable objects (candy or other rewards), give continual support ("I'm here. There is nothing here to harm you."), or train the child to relax (deep breathing, muscle relaxation exercises).

The first step in a desensitization program might be having the child watch a fearless peer perform the feared behavior several times.

ADDITIONAL READING

Krumboltz, J.D. and Krumboltz, H.B. *Changing Children's Behavior*. Prentice-Hall, Englewood Cliffs, New Jersey, 1972. See section on desensitization of fears.

ENCOURAGING

To help the young soul, to add energy, inspire hope, and blow the coals into a useful flame; to redeem defeat by new thought and firm action, this, though, not easy, is the work of divine men.

Emerson

All children need words of parental encouragement in order to do their best. Children who are naturally shy or who have become disheartened because of repeated failures particularly need this assistance. Encouragement means giving children the courage, hope, and confidence that they can face and deal with all of life's tasks — especially the ones that are dangerous, difficult, or painful. Parental encouragement serves as an ego-booster when children are confronted with difficult tasks or stressful events. It helps a child develop self-confidence, initiative, and perseverence.

In encouraging children, some of the attitudes that you will want to convey to them are:

1. You are basically a competent, courageous person.
2. You are the type of child who won't give up.
3. I am confident that you can take hurts and setbacks, learn from them, and eventually overcome them.
4. I won't ask you to do anything that is beyond your abilities.
5. A reasonably good effort on your part will please me.
6. You can make of life what you will.

Guidelines for Encouraging Children

The following are some ways to offer encouragement to children:

1. *Urgings.* You can urge a child or give the needed push to do something by saying: "Come on, do it! Do it now!"
2. *Express Confidence.* If you really believe that a child can do it, and you fully expect him to, you might say: "You can do it, I know you can!" and "You're going to do it now!"
3. *Coaxing.* Use soothing words, humor, or a pleasant manner to persuade: "It's really very easy once you're used to it." "Everyone's afraid of it at first."

4. *Pleading.* Occasionally, you might give an earnest appeal, e.g., "Please try it! Oh, please, please do it."

5. *Provide Information.* Give relevant facts to dispel irrational beliefs. Research has shown that it is best to give *specific* facts, e.g., "That bee won't sting you!" rather than general truths, e.g., "Bees won't harm people."

6. *Challenging.* Make it seem like a challenge, e.g., "Don't let life defeat you."

7. *Praise.* Comment upon child's past success and how persistent or courageous he was in past situations. Comment on parts of the task he has already gotten right, minimize his errors, and indicate how the child should proceed to be successful. Also, praise the times the child gives a good effort but is not successful. You might say, for instance, "I want you to think about this. Sometimes you'll be successful in life and sometimes you won't. The important thing is to try your best. I'm very proud of you today since you did your best in trying out for the cheerleader team even though you didn't win." (When a child fails, you might also recount a time when you failed at something as a child. In this way, the child will not feel unique in suffering adversity.)

8. *Proverbs.* Offer one of your favorite maxims to bolster the child's resolve: e.g., "Nothing ventured, nothing gained.", "Practice makes perfect.", "No life is so hard that you can't make it easier by the way you take it."

9. *Persuasive Appeals.* Verbally appeal to the child's self-respect or desire for recognition, e.g., "Your teacher is going to love this when you are finished."

10. *Teamwork.* Initially, you and the child might do the task together and then you would gradually fade out.

11. *Physical Presence.* Just having a parent there when faced with a severely stressful task can be comforting to a child.

12. *Touch.* Sometimes verbal encouragement is insufficient. You have to take the child's hand and lead him to the feared object. Be verbally reassuring as you do this.

13. *Modeling.* Try to model courage and determination in overcoming obstacles in your own life.

14. *Sparingly.* If you overdo encouragement, your child will not attempt anything difficult without your help.

Discussion

Encouragement must be based on a sincere faith and confidence in humanity, i.e., an inner conviction that your children have the ability to actively shape their own lives rather than being passive victims of fate. It is generally recognized now that we get from children what we expect. If we have little faith in children and expect them to give up easily or fold under extreme pressure or calamity, they will rarely disappoint us. Thus, even though your child may initially fail and be discouraged, you must not lose hope. Rather you should transmit to this child your confidence that he or she will one day learn to overcome the obstacle. Words alone will not give this faith to a child, but somehow the child will understand it if you really believe it. Kids truly need to develop a kind of positive expectancy that they are going to do well in life and not be overcome by adversity or difficulty.

ATTRIBUTING POSITIVE QUALITIES

Faith is to believe what we do not see, and its reward is to see and enjoy what we believe.

St. Augustine

A blend of encouragement, positive suggestion, and persuasion is the act of attributing to children a positive quality or behavior, when there is only the slightest evidence that they actually possess it. In other words, you attempt to inspire children to behave in a positive way by suggesting that they are already behaving that way to some degree. Thus, you might remark to a shy, passive child, "Boy, you really stuck up for your rights last week!", or "You know, the way you just held your ground with your girl friend means that you can't be pushed around so easily anymore. You're really asserting yourself lately!" or "You really were very courageous in getting that shot from the doctor. You stopped crying right away, even though it was still painful." (In reality, there was only very minimal evidence for self-assertive acts at these times.)

To a messy child, you might say the following:

"Our family is clean and does not litter."
"I appreciate your picking up that paper."
"You really lined those books up in a well ordered row."
"Your room seems cleaner lately."
"I know you want to keep things neat and orderly so that you can find them."
"At heart, you're really an orderly person."
"You really keep your art supplies neat and clean."

If you keep repeating the message that the child is a particular kind of person, it should eventually take hold in the child's mind. As a result, the child should not only begin making self-attributions in the same vein, but gain in self-confidence and positive self-regard.

Discussion

The average child can be readily led if you have his confidence and if you show him that you respect him for some kind of ability. So you can improve a certain ability or trait in a child by acting as if this behavior was already one of his special skills or characteristics. Give a child a good reputation to live up to and he will work hard rather than disappoint you. In this regard, studies have shown that repeatedly attributing to fifth graders the ability or motivation to be neat proved more effective in improving their performance than trying to persuade them that they should do better and not litter. Attribution seems to be effective because it disguises persuasive intent and does not devalue a child by indicating he should be something he is not.

In using attributions, care should be taken to make them not too discrepant from a child's ability, i.e., don't label a child good in math who is generally a slow learner. You must be able to point to some behaviors which confirm your attributions, or you will lose credibility in your child's eyes. Once you have a positive image of what a child is capable of becoming — despite past behaviors — then treat the child as if he is already what you would like him to be. But you have got to believe that the infrequent good behaviors represent who the child really is. Children see themselves primarily through their parents' eyes and they depend on you for a larger vision of themselves.

IMPLANT VALUES

He who merely knows right principles is not equal to him who loves them.

Confucius

Principles last forever; but special rules pass away with the things and conditions to which they refer.

Seeley

It is likely that, apart from discipline, the aspect of childrearing that parents feel most insecure in and uncertain of is the development of moral principles in children. One reason is that society's values have changed so rapidly in recent years, as have the personal value systems of many parents. Nonetheless, children still look to their parents for an evaluation of the goodness and badness of behavior. Consequently, it is important for you to communicate some well-defined values which will help them govern their behavior. Values help children integrate their personality and live in harmony with others. Any definite beliefs based upon ethical or altruistic principles will serve to act as constructive influences.

Perhaps the most important principle to teach a child is to love, i.e., an approach to people which tends to be considerate, cooperative, kind, and empathic. Time and again, encourage children to take another's viewpoint and to practice the golden rule. This will instill the universal principle of equality (equal worth of all men) and reciprocity (do unto others as. . .). Other universal values that should be taught are honesty, industriousness, justice and charity.

Be enthusiastic in explaining and discussing basic values with a child rather than presenting do's and don'ts in a cold, grim manner. Be positive in your approach and teach a child to act moral out of love and caring for others rather than fear of punishment. Show a child that to lead a good life out of heart-felt principles is ennobling and joyful. Apart from just intellectually knowing what is right, a child should feel what is desirable, so emphasize the joy of giving and caring.

Before we can confidently teach a child moral principles, we must clarify and establish our own set of values. A child's moral dilemmas at each stage of his development will serve as catalysts for you to redefine and reaffirm your own moral commitments. Once you are comfortable with your own values, be alert to situations where you can teach them to your child. As children mature, be sure to explain to them the reasons you hold certain values and be open to discussion. You must also allow the children the right to dissent and choose their own values when they are mature enough. Exposing them to the differing value systems of others as they develop will enable your children to make more informed choices. The value clarifying skill described in the next section will also be helpful in this regard.

Many parents either have not developed a strong personal value system, or are reluctant to impart values to their children because they want the children to form their own moral standards. In these cases, the children will be more susceptible to value implantation from sources outside the home, i.e., charlatans, radical religious sects, and their peer group. The prime responsibility to help children form their moral judgments belongs to parents and they must be willing to accept this.

Since a child's character is well established by age ten, parents should be continually reinforcing moral actions in their children from an early age. By rewarding and penalizing good and bad acts, you help the child establish a sense of right and wrong and the value of self and others. Children must be held responsible for their actions. Rather than accepting excuses, ask the child to evaluate whether his behavior was helpful to himself or others. Give victim-centered punishment which helps the child tune in to the plight of those he has hurt.

In addition to teaching and rewarding moral behavior when it occurs, you should work hard at modeling moral actions by your daily behavior. Morals are more caught than taught, so set a positive example. You can set a high standard by such acts as avoiding cheating on your income taxes or telling "white lies" ("Tell the person on the phone that I'm not in.") Rather, model altruistic behavior, i.e., donate blood and give money or work for local charities. Take every opportunity to allow your children to assist you when you help others in need. Even more important than how to treat others is how you treat your own children. If your children feel wanted, accepted, loved and feel that they receive consistent, just, and understanding discipline, they will most likely treat others in the same moral vein.

Discussion

In a fairly recent survey, more than 2,000 adolescents responded to a question asking what they would like changed in their home life.* *More religion* was one of the three most frequent answers. (The other two were better communication and more time together as a family.) Rather than blindly accepting religious beliefs, the teenagers said they wanted to discuss these values with their parents and make the values relevant to their daily lives. A large number of adolescents today clearly have a deep desire to find a transcendental, spiritual meaning to their lives.

VALUE CLARIFYING

Man, know thyself; all wisdom centers there.

Young

Although it is generally too late to begin teaching basic values to teenagers, you can help them further consider, affirm, and act on their values.

One way to help your teenagers become more aware of their basic values is to ask them questions about their fundamental beliefs. These questions should stimulate their thinking about personal values and how they relate to their daily lives.

Among the value focusing questions you might ask are:

"Was what you did helpful to you?"
"Is this something you prize?"
"Does it make you feel good when you do that?"
"What brings you the most happiness in life?"
"Is this something that you yourself want to do?"
"How do you know if this is right?"

*Bienvenu, M.J. *Parent-Teenager Communication.* Public Affairs Pamphlet, New York, 1970.

"This seems to mean a lot to you."

"Do you think people should always tell the truth, no matter what?"

"Who are your heroes? Who are the people you admire the most? Why do you admire them?"

Another way to help a teenager develop values is to openly and fully discuss moral conflict situations which arise in daily life, e.g., right to life, right to die, mercy killing. In these value clarifying discussions, both sides of a moral issue should be presented to ensure that all moral decisions are based upon informed choice.

Discussion

In value clarifying, no attempt is made to teach new values, pressure a child to accept your values, or evaluate a child's values. The goal is simply to assist your children to delineate and clarify for themselves the guiding beliefs in their lives and to consider whether these beliefs are reflected in their actions.

ADDITIONAL READING

Simon, S.B., Howe, L.W., and Kirschenbaum, H. *Values Clarification,* Hart Publishing Company, New York, 1972.

RELABELING

No man was ever so much deceived by another, as by himself.

Greville

Children often tend to describe certain antisocial behaviors in a positive light. From watching cowboy and Indian movies on TV, for instance, they may infer that it is heroic to kill Indians; from viewing a number of cartoons, they may come to feel that it is OK to be physically aggressive towards others. Similarly, from associating with their peer group, boys may believe that it is feminine, weak, or stupid to show helpful or considerate behavior. The task of the parent, then, is to constantly reverse their thinking about the positive-negative value of certain behaviors by means of a relabeling procedure. You should refer to any type of helping behaviors as strong, mature, and powerful, while describing or labeling all hurting and dishonest behaviors as weak, immature, or cowardly.

In using this procedure, you should take care not to downgrade a child's motivation to be strong and courageous; rather, redirect this desire into socially desirable channels. By your words, you indicate to children that you believe that a person who is really brave and strong helps others rather than hurts them. Thus, don't let your children get away with whitewashing antisocial, self-defeating behaviors by describing them in exciting or romantic terms. For example, if your child says it's "cool" to "rip off" candy from a store, you would call this being sneaky or stupid, because it's stealing what belongs to another. If a child says he thinks he might give someone a knuckle sandwich, you might relabel by saying, "You mean you're thinking of acting like a hothead or a bully by physically hitting someone with your fist and hurting them?"

By using euphemisms for deviant acts, children and adults try to lessen or eliminate their culpability in the acts. "Ripping off," for example, implies that stealing consists of taking by strength something that is sticking out or extended to you, whereas the word stealing denotes the dishonest and secretive taking of something that belongs to another. Like children, most of us believe we are good and rarely blame ourselves for anything. Instead, we use various strategies to defend our self-esteem and rationalize away the guilt. H.R. Haldeman, for instance, steadfastly proclaimed his innocence in the Watergate affair, despite the overwhelming evidence to the contrary. To be sure, he probably never said to himself, "Bob, you're going to commit a crime now and obstruct justice." Rather, as John Dean stated, Haldeman and others used euphemisms such as "containing" Watergate, keeping the defendents "on the reservation," and coming up with the right public relations "scenario." Don't let your children deceive themselves by whitewashing or romanticizing their deviant acts. Help them to redefine their acts in a realistic, responsibility-accepting manner.

If your teenager attempts to minimize his act of vandalism, for example, by saying he was just fooling around or having a little fun, you might more accurately define it as defacing and seriously marring property that belongs to another. Frequent use of the redefining-relabeling procedure should influence your children to develop appropriate attitudes and values as well as honest, realistic terms for antisocial behaviors.

ADDITIONAL READING

Vorrath, H.H. and Brendtro, L.K. *Positive Peer Culture.* Aldine, Chicago, Illinois, 1974. An excellent description of this technique.

REVERSING

It's been said that children have 1,000 reasons for failure but not one valid excuse. A common excuse of children is to shift blame onto others, e.g., "He started it!"

Since children are quite skilled at giving excuses and projecting responsibility for their misdeeds onto others, parents must develop an equally effective technique for shifting the responsibility back when it belongs with the child. Only when a child feels responsible for his actions can he learn from his experiences and resolve his difficulties. A crucial first step for children if they are to change maladaptive behavior is to admit some responsibility or culpability for it.

The following verbal interactions illustrate how you might use the reversing technique:

Child: I got into trouble at school today because the teacher is so boring and can't teach.

Parent: You mean that all kids with poor teachers get into trouble?

Child: I hit him because he called me a name!

Parent: I can understand that. I wonder why she called you a name. Could you have done something that annoyed her?

Child: The other kids made me do it.

Parent: You mean to say that you're a puppet on strings and that everybody else pulls your strings but yourself?

Discussion

Effective use of the reversing technique will depend not only on your skill in drawing out of children their role in a conflict, but also your tone of voice, your interest in, and concern for the children, and your attitude (one of wanting to help children by assisting them to see the real source of their difficulty).

ADDITIONAL READING

Vorrath, H.H. and Brendtro, L.K. *Positive Peer Culture.* Aldine, Chicago, Illinois, 1974. A discussion of the reversing technique.

COACHING

Coaching means giving children special instruction or guidance to prepare them to cope with future events. By thinking and practicing things through in advance, children will be more confident and skillful when new or difficult events actually occur.

Foretelling

Children should be helped to anticipate what to expect in new and potentially fearful situations and to prepare for them. Foretelling what to expect and how to act by detailed explanations, coupled with reassurance, will contribute a great deal towards minimizing the shock of the unknown and unexpected. For example, before giving a child a needle, a doctor should state what is going to happen next: "I'm going to give you a needle which will hurt a little at first. But I know you're going to be brave about it."

Before going on a new trip, say something like, "Let's talk about our trip to Disneyland. What do you think it will be like? What are your feelings about the trip? Is anybody excited about it? Does anyone feel a little uneasy or lonely when they think about being away from home?"

In a similar manner, parents can prepare children for hospital trips, a new baby, a divorce, camping, or a new school. There are many excellent books available to help parents forewarn their children about many of these experiences.

"What if" Game

Another way to prepare a child for possible problem situations is to play the "what if" game. You might ask, for example, "*What* is the thing to do *if* a complete stranger comes up to you and asks you to go for a ride in his car?" or "What is the thing to do if one of your balls rolls out into the street?"

Preparatory Experiences

Try to give children some preparatory experiences to introduce them to future change and challenge. Thus, if your son will soon be going away to college, you might help him prepare for this rather drastic change by insisting that he have some prior experience living away from home, perhaps as a summer camp counselor or with a relative. Be sure there is opportunity for supervision and feedback in the preparatory experience. As a further illustration, before sending a child to five-day a week kindergarten, you might enroll the child in a two-or-three-day a week nursery school program.

Behavior Rehearsal

A child who is experiencing interpersonal difficulties can often be helped by your playing the role of the person the child is having difficulty with and acting out the conflict situation with the child. Role playing or behavior rehearsal tends to change a discussion from a strictly intellectual level to a real feeling and experiential level.

If, for instance, your child has become very fearful of a teacher, you might act out the teacher's typical behavior while the child plays herself. The goal of the play acting is to assist the child to respond to the teacher in a more appropriate manner, i.e., less fearful and anxious. Thus, after your child has responded in her typical fearful way, you might suggest that she try responding in a more assertive but still respectful manner. In the event that your child just does not know how to act more assertively, you would assume the role of the child and act out a proper response to the teacher. At this time, you might suggest that your child play the role of the teacher. By this role reversal, you will be encouraging your child to develop a greater degree of empathy, i.e., the ability to experience events from another's perspective.

Young children especially seem to enjoy role playing, although it adapts well to any age. With younger children, you will find it advantageous to use puppets and dolls during the role playing.

In addition to resolving interpersonal conflicts, role playing can be used to prepare children for complex social situations. For example, if your child is afraid to go to the store alone, you might play the game of "going to the store" in which each element of shopping — selecting the desired item, taking it to the counter, paying the cashier, and counting the change — can be rehearsed in a pleasant, relaxed manner with your help.

Similarly, if your child is experiencing difficulty handling teasing from other children, you might have the child tease you while you model a variety of adaptive responses, including:

Ignore the teasing, saying:
"So what."
"Thanks for telling me my fault."
"Why pick on me?"
"That's really a mean thing to say."

Then, you might ask your child to practice saying these responses while you tease him.

FOSTER SELF-RELIANCE

What is the best government? — that which teaches us to govern ourselves.

Goethe

Self-reliance or *autonomy* can be defined as the desire to control one's actions and be free of external control. The goal is to be a self-regulating, inner-directed, separate human being. A self-reliant person takes initiative, overcomes obstacles by himself, and wants to do things on his own. One of your tasks as a parent is to make your child autonomous as quickly as possible and thereby work yourself out of a job. This will not be easy, however, since it is more natural for parents to overprotect a child in keeping with the desire to feel important and needed. You have to constantly remind yourself to let go and step back from the center of a child's world into the background.

Gradually Widen the Circle of Freedom

The goal of self-reliance can only be achieved if a child is given more and more opportunities to explore, experiment, and, within limits, make his own mistakes. One sign of good parents is that they don't do for a child what he can do for himself. From an early age, they encourage children to think and do things for themselves with messages such as, "I expect you to do that for yourself. Somehow or other, you'll do it even though it's hard at first."

The ability to function as an autonomous human being should be developed slowly over the course of many years. Granting more and more independence to children to do things for themselves should be a gradual and continuous process as a child grows older and matures. This gradual process for normal children is illustrated in the following diagram.

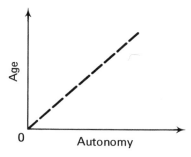

This can also be called the law of diminishing structure, i.e., as a child grows older you impose fewer rules and restrictions. Some parents tend to keep children protected and dependent until they reach the age of 16 and then they expect the children to become mature adults almost overnight.

A more reasonable approach is to gradually increase children's level of self-reliance by steadily giving them more and more freedom and independence. For example, children should normally be given increased freedom with age to manage their own affairs, e.g., care of personal possessions, use of free time, and personal appearance. They should also be given fewer and fewer restrictions in such matters as the hour they retire at night and the distance they can travel away from home.

In the final analysis, a reasonable balance be⁺ween freedom and restriction in a child's life is the essence of discipline and the hallmark of effective parenting. A common pitfall in this regard is that parents tend to be unaware of a child's readiness for the next higher level of development. As a result, they tend to be slow in granting independence and freedom.

Encourage Decision Making from an Early Age

Apart from granting more and more freedom of action, parents should be developing, from an early age, the child's ability to make decisions and accept responsibility for the consequences of those decisions. When you permit children to make decisions, they find out about alternatives and what it is like to make a choice and live with it.

Encourage decision making by saying: "It's your decision."; "It's up to you."; "Whatever you think; it's your choice." Once children make a decision, they must learn to accept responsibility for the consequences of their choices. Thus, if a child decides to spend his allowance the first day he receives it, then he must experience what it is like to do without money for the rest of the week. If he orders a hamburger, he must either eat it or go hungry.

Allow children to make a decision when they can both anticipate and evaluate the probable consequences of alternate courses of action. Though very young children are capable of making personal decisions (e.g., "Do you want your bread plain or toasted?"; "Do you want to wear your blue or red pants?"; "You have a choice of remaining here and being quiet, or leaving. You decide."), parents must be careful to allow children only those decisions that are appropriate to their age or level of maturity. You would not, for instance, give teenagers complete freedom to choose the high school they will attend when they have insufficient knowledge of basic curriculums or vocational requirements. Nor would you send a child out alone to select his clothes until he had knowledge of quality, styles, and the value of money. Apart from soliciting a child's opinion in these matters, an effective way to encourage them to have a voice, but not the complete say, is to limit their choices. In taking a child shopping, for example, you might show her two articles of clothing preselected by you for quality and price, and then ask her to make the final choice. In regard to choice of high schools, you might say, "Howard, your mother and I have determined that we can afford to send you to either Jefferson or Hamilton High School. Both are high quality schools that offer the type of curriculum you are interested in. The final choice is up to you." The wisdom of offering limited choices to children is reflected in the saying of the poet Robert Frost: "Freedom moves easily in harness." Of course, as they mature, children should be given more and more opportunities to have the complete say in decisions affecting their lives.

Avoid Psychological Bondage

Some parents believe that their role in life is to almost completely sacrifice themselves and their personal pleasures for the sake of the children. In return, they expect their children to give them a great deal of love, devotion, and gratitude.

Parental love, in these instances, is not made a joy but rather a profound duty and unending obligation. By their sacrifices and grim existence, some parents try to put their children in psychological bondage for the rest of their lives. Being obliged to love someone is a difficult burden to carry. It is well known that marriages arranged because of duty rather than love stand little chance of success. The same principle applies when a child is bound to his parents out of guilt rather than love and genuine liking. To bind your child by guilt, to be sure to remind him at every opportunity how much you have done for him, and at what sacrifice to yourself. Never become a self-reliant person. Look to your children for the *main* source of your happiness, rather than to self or spouse.

Suffering and making sacrifices for children are part of the role of being a parent. In compensation, there are many joys to be found in raising children. Weighing the good and the bad, most parents admit that it's worth it to have children. One could speak of parents being indebted to children for adding joy and fulfillment to the parents' lives. Rather than speaking of debts and obligations, it seems best to speak of a balanced ledger wherein the needs of both parties have been met and all concerned are the better for it. The enduring bonds between parent and child should be those of love and affection rather than guilt or indebtedness.

Mothers, in particular, should be on guard to avoid the "Portnoy's Complaint syndrome" of attempting to vicariously, obsessively, and possessively live their lives through their children. In general, one avoids this by actively pursuing procedures that enhance self-awareness, self-development, and self-liking, i.e., becoming a fully actualized person, and by cultivating your relationship with your spouse, relatives, and friends.

DEVELOP CONFIDENCE IN CHILDREARING

Studies of parents who have well-adjusted children have shown that they believe that they have the ability to exert a positive influence on the behavior of their children. All parents need to have a conviction or firm belief that they are right in what they are doing as parents, that it will work out. Every time you make a mistake or your child fails, you've got to admit it and accept the fact that it's going to happen thousands of times, but that you are going to succeed in the long run.

Parental expectation in the area of discipline is a very important force. The parent who is confident in his own authority expects appropriate self-control in his children and has fewer disciplinary problems. You must be certain that you are right in making the expectations that a child will behave in a certain way. Unless parents are convinced they are right, they will not have the necessary confidence in what they are doing, and this lack of confidence or guilt is easily sensed by children so that the desired results will be more difficult to achieve. The detection of ambivalence or guilt by a child will keep alive the hope that the present set of rules might be changed through stubbornness, sympathy-seeking, or other means. When you are committed to winning and succeeding, then the child will see this and comply more readily.

The simplest and soundest method of deciding on the best course to follow with children is to decide first what the final result is to be, and what kind of person you are trying to produce? What behaviors do you want in a child? Do you want a child who always does what he is told without questioning? Or do you want a self-reliant individual who thinks for himself?

If we think only of the present, we are likely to use techniques which are easiest and produce the quickest results. When we think in terms of the future, we tend to use different methods and stress different values. So plan a philosophy of parenting based on long term goals. The more you have thought out your approach, the more confident you will be in applying it. The less vague (I want good children.) and the more specific you are in your goals (I want my children to be self-directed, empathic, and considerate of others, knowing and valuing their uniqueness, having high standards, happy and fun-loving, and so on.), the more effective you will be.

Other ways of gaining confidence in your childrearing ability include reading books, taking courses, attending lectures, conferring and consulting with other parents who have children the same age as yours, and forming parent discussion groups. Family counseling or therapy is still another alternative.

Apart from the above, it is reassuring to know that common sense goes a long way in childrearing. Even more comforting is the fact that kids are remarkably resilient when it comes to psychological bruises so that you can make many mistakes with them and they will still come out OK. What seems of crucial importance is your basic relationship with the child. The more children feel your love and concern, the more your mistakes will roll off their backs.

SETTING PERSONAL GOALS

Helping Children Set Goals for Self-Improvement

Most children want to improve their behavior, but they usually need help in establishing concrete, specific goals or objectives which point the way toward constructive change. Having a clear goal to strive for gives direction to one's behavior and is thus a strong motivating force. It helps a child become a doer rather than a complainer.

Parents can assist children in translating their nonspecific complaints about themselves into clear, specific goals. Be realistic and help children set moderately difficult goals that are just slightly beyond their reach. Set the goals high enough to be a challenge but within view so they can be realized quickly.

When a child describes his weakness as a general trait or characteristic, such as "I'm too shy," you should listen carefully and try to understand what this weakness means to your child and under what circumstances it occurs. Get as much information as you can; try for facts rather than opinions. By this procedure, you should be able to help the child restate his vague complaint into the form of a specific, concrete goal which states what the child wants to happen. Thus, the "I'm too shy" statement might be translated to "You feel shy because you haven't been able to initiate conversation with your camp counselor, and you want to be able to do this."

A child's complaint, "Nobody likes me. I'm no good." may be converted into "You feel lonely and left out because you have no friends and you want to have at least one friend play with you on a regular basis." This goal then becomes translated, with the child's help, into the first step of an action program: "The first step, then, is for you to invite one or two of your classmates over to play this weekend." In this way, you have stated the problem so it seems soluble (not so big as to seem overwhelming) and you phrased it so that the child owns the problem (what the child can do to solve it) rather than focusing on what others have done or can do about the problem.

Once a goal has been pinpointed, your child needs to make a final decision or commitment to act. Encourage the decision making process by asking, "Will you do it?" Get a verbal statement reflecting a determination to act. Then discuss the means of implementing the goal, i.e., who will do what and when. Check with your child each week to see how the plan is working. If you fail to check with the child on a regular basis, the firm resolve is likely to go the way of most New Year's Resolutions. Incidentally, just as the New Year is a good time to make personal resolutions, other changes in a child's life can be capitalized on to motivate needed behavior changes. For example, you might say, "Now that you'll be starting Nursery School, we'll have to help you learn to go to the potty by yourself." or "Now that you'll be going to first grade soon, don't you think it's time to work on your thumbsucking habit?"

Parental Goals for a Child

In disciplining a child, parents are much better off when they set as their goal changing one misdeed of the child at a time. So avoid getting upset and complaining about a gunny sack full of grievances, such as: "You only think of yourself. . .you never help your mother . . .never do anything to help around the house. . .you only gripe and complain. . .you never show any respect for others. . .you do as you please and come in when you like. . .I don't know what's the matter with you!"

Research evidence suggests that when you try to change a child's general misbehavior or bad attitude — consisting of a wide range of inappropriate behaviors — you get the least improvement for your efforts. So it seems best to focus on one, specific behavior of your child that you want to change, e.g., staying out late at night. Try to set a goal that is observable and measurable so that you and your child will be able to assess progress or lack of progress in reaching the goal. Finally, ask your child to make a small step forward rather than a giant leap. As a general principle, think small in striving for a behavioral change in a child and reward large. Don't expect too much change too quickly, but be persistent in resisting the child's efforts to avoid changing.

ADDITIONAL READING

Patterson, G.R. and Gullion, M.E. *Living With Children.* Research Press, 1968.

HELPING CHILDREN THINK POSITIVELY

Men are disturbed not by the things which happen, but by their opinions about the things.

Epictetus

Research has indicated that many negative feelings of children, such as anger, anxiety, and apathy, are triggered off by irrational thoughts and beliefs. For example, if a child thinks to himself that he is a bad, worthless person, and that there is no hope, then he will feel sad and depressed. If a child feels he failed an exam because of stupidity rather than poor study habits, then he is also likely to become depressed. Sources of irrational thoughts in children are their tendency to overgeneralize, e.g., one mistake means stupidity; their proclivity for dichotomous, black-and-white thinking, e.g., "Others are either friends or enemies."; and their tendency to overreact and make things worse than they are, e.g., "This is terrible! It's a disaster."

Parents can help children with their irrational beliefs by bringing out into the open and into conscious awareness the thoughts that they are quietly telling themselves. Some of the common irrational beliefs that people have are:

1. The belief that they must be perfectly successful at whatever they do and never fail, or else it would be awful, terrible, and catastrophic;
2. The belief that they must be loved, liked, or admired by everyone they meet;
3. The belief that nothing bad or unpleasant should ever happen to them;
4. The idea that they must be given whatever they desire, immediately.

Once a child's irrational ideas have been brought to the surface, then you and your child will be in a better position to replace these ideas with more realistic, rational thoughts. Thus, for a child who believes he is bad and worthless, you would point out the things he has done that are good and worthwhile. You would also explain that even if he had never done anything good in his life you would still love him and he would be worthwhile to you.

If a child suffers a minor crisis, e.g., forgets her lines in a play, help her realize this isn't the great calamity that she thinks it is. Assist her to gain perspective on the setback and take it in her stride. Point out that no one expects her to be perfect and that the event in no way diminishes her worth as a person in your eyes. Point out that the important thing is not the mishap, but what the child is saying to herself about the event. It is not the stresses in life that determine your character, but how you react to them. It's not what people think about you that counts, but what you think and know about yourself that matters.

In addition to diminishing negative thinking, you should endeavor to help your child develop positive thinking. Positive thinking is based on the fact that there is more than one way of looking at things. You can look out the window, for example, and see a partly cloudy day (negative view) or look out and see a partly sunny day (positive view). Both are equally correct. One view is life-enhancing, the other is life-defeating. A positive attitude and can do spirit will ensure that good things happen. Thus, don't let children start the day by telling themselves that they are going to have a bad day because that is exactly what will happen. Help children replace the negative "vibes" with more positive thinking by telling themselves that they are going to have a good day each morning. Optimism and enthusiasm will lift them up to peak performance and help overcome difficulties. Of course, the best way to teach a positive orientation is to model this behavior yourself.

ADDITIONAL READING

Ellis, Albert. *A Guide To Rational Living.* Wilshire Book Co., 1961. Guidelines for identifying and overcoming irrational ideas.

Fay, Allen. *I Can If I Want To.*

Peale, Norman Vincent. *The Power of Positive Thinking.*

ENCOURAGE POSITIVE IMAGERY

There is a well-known psychological law which states that images or mental pictures tend to produce the physical conditions and external acts that correspond to them. As the noted psychologist William James once said, "Every image has in itself a motor element." Therefore, parents should play a role in helping children develop their imaginal abilities. For example, if your children are upset after experiencing a nightmare, you might help them relax by encouraging them to imagine a pleasant scene, e.g., resting on the beach after swimming. You might also help them to picture pleasant images by reading them a favorite story.

On another occasion, you might encourage your children to picture in their minds, as vividly as possible, how their life would be different if they developed a strong will to enable them to stop their temper tantrums. You would ask the children to imagine themselves as having attained this self-control or willpower. Then ask them to describe in detail the picture they have formed in their minds. A related procedure would be to ask them to draw a picture of this mental scene. Similarly, you might ask children to draw pictures portraying what they want to be when they grow up, or to draw a self-portrait of how they picture their ideal self. In this connection, a child's action-drawing of his conception of an ideal parent might activate your own fantasies in a positive way.

Discussion

Fantasy can also be used to offer immediate substitute gratification for events. Thus, if your child is hungry and there is no food immediately available, you might suggest that he imagine his favorite food, e.g., a "Big Mac." This subsittute pleasure may tide the child over a difficult waiting period.

It is a well-known psychological principle that fantasy can bring substitute satisfactions to people. In this regard, four types of wish-fulfilling fantasies have been identified:

1. Display — you perform a feat which brings applause.
2. Rescue — you perform a heroic act which brings you the devotion of the rescued person.
3. Grandeur — you are a member of royalty or some deity.
4. Homage — you accomplish some unusual feat for an admirer.

CLARIFYING CHILDREN'S ROLE

All parents should examine and discuss the role and function of children in their lives. In delineating the role of children, you should consider why you had children and what your expectations are for them.

One way of accomplishing this is to sit down with your spouse and list what you believe to be the rights and responsibilities of children, as well as your wishes and expectations for them.

One couple, listed the following:

Children's Rights
- Freely express their ideas.
- Be loved and wanted.
- Follow own interests.
- Develop own values.
- Be educated (college, then they are on their own).
- Individual attention (one hour with each parent per week).
- High quality medical and dental care.
- Clean clothing of good quality.
- Privacy (time alone, own phone).
- Right to disagree with parents.
- Have voice in decisions affecting them.

Children's Responsibilities
- Help with housework when able.
- Respect and obey parents.
- Live in accord with society's laws and mores until mature enough to make informed dissent.
- Be considerate of others.
- Develop own talents.
- Work hard and to the best of their ability on tasks.
- Be doers rather than complainers.

Long-term Wishes and Expectations for Children
- Love and be devoted to parents.
- Be source of comfort and security to parents in old age.
- Carry on family name.

- Achieve more than parents.
- Be source of joy and delight.
- Be a companion or confidant to parents.
- Never be source of embarrassment.

In contrast to the above long term goals, most experts agree that the goal of parents in this country should be to raise children who can function well in a democratic society, who are kind, reasonably altruistic, cooperative and considerate of others, effective problem-solvers, and independent and self-sufficient, yet able to enter into close personal relationships. Once you know your goals, you will find that there are some childrearing practices that are more likely to achieve them than others.

Discussion

The clearer you are about what you expect from children, the clearer the children will be about their role. Be sure to communicate early and repeatedly to children what you expect. In some homes, you will see displayed a children's "Bill of Rights" and a children's "Bill of Responsibilities." Once you have articulated norms which define how children are expected to act in your family, you should consider whether your actual practices belie your beliefs, e.g., do you expect children to be more autonomous as they grow older but refuse to allow them more freedom and continue to offer advice when it is not needed; do you believe children should freely express themselves but you actually practice: "Children should be seen but not heard."

Similarly, you may say that you expect your child to be educated, but you may make no provisions for your child's college expenses and you may make no effort to continue your own education. In regard to academic expectations, research studies have shown that children are more likely to have positive attitudes towards school if they perceive their parents as wanting them to be good students and expecting them to go far in school.

In communicating your expectations to children, be sure you don't keep raising the ante so that as a child meets one standard you raise it higher, and then higher so that it seems nothing will please you. Such perfectionistic and ill-defined standards are likely to discourage children or make them very insecure and anxious. Such an attitude is illustrated by the parent who, when a child brings home a report card with all A's and one B, overlooks the A's and proceeds to criticize the B.

Perfectionist parents are usually too critical in that they expect too much and are always finding fault. They tend to overlook small positive acts and focus too much on children's deficiencies.

FEEDING BACK REALITY

Children need feedback from their parents to validate the psychological growth and progress they are making. Rather than taking progress for granted, you should point out to a child that he is able to do certain things that he was not able to do before. For example, you might comment, "John, you know it really wasn't too long ago that you really used to get upset a lot. Remember those times when you would yell and kick and scream? Now you hardly ever get upset like you used to and you seem to have much better control over your emotions."

The purpose of substantiating or validating a child's progress is not so much to impress him with your approval, but to help him realize that there is clear and objective cause for him to be proud of himself.

A child's lack of progress should also be noted in a calm, matter-of-fact tone, e.g., "Margaret, you're biting your nails again."

Discussion

Noteworthy is the fact that studies have shown that children do not naturally develop a basis for realistic self-evaluation. Rather, they tend to be overly harsh in their evaluations and tend to give themselves fewer positive evaluations than adults would judge warranted in the same situation. In giving a child feedback about his task performance, be sure to include positive as well as negative feedback. Some adults take good work for granted and fail to report it to children.

Recording

A useful tool to help you provide feedback is to keep a written account of the frequency of occurrence of a child's behavior. Careful observation and recording by parents of the incidence of a child's misbehavior will not only provide information as to the seriousness of a misdeed, but also will help establish a reference point for evaluating progress. Since a child's behavior change is typically slow and gradual, a systematic frequency count will reveal slow progress that might otherwise be overlooked.

Simple checklists or charts for recording the frequency of a child's behavior can be made by parents. For example, if you wanted to measure how aggressive your child is to his siblings, you would first redefine the problem behavior in more precise, concrete terms, e.g., aggression might be defined as hitting, kicking, or roughly handling a sibling. One parent would then set aside a period each day to record the frequency of the misbehavior. The recording period would be when the misbehavior is usually at its peak, e.g., 4 to 5 P.M. when the children play together in the house. The parent then tallies the frequency of occurrence of the target behavior as follows:

	M	T	W	Th	F	S	S	Total (week one)
Number of times observed:	𝍤𝍤 II	𝍤𝍤	𝍤𝍤	𝍤𝍤 I	IIII	III	II	32

You might want to show a child a graph depicting his progress over a series of weeks. A chart or graph can be worth a thousand words.

In lieu of actual counting, you can use a five point behavior rating scale to measure progress, e.g., Child hits siblings: All the times he is near them____; Frequently (about 75% of the times)____; Occasionally (about 50% of the times)____; Seldom (about 25% of the times)____; Never____. Rating scales are, of course, less accurate than actually counting behaviors.

Discussion

Often just explaining to your child why you are observing (you are disturbed about his hitting, kicking and pushing his brother) and posting the recording sheet will be enough to reduce the frequency of the misbehavior. In other words, your concern and the daily feedback provided by the recordings will serve to help the child control his behavior.

Your careful observation of a child's behavior will also assist you to determine the circumstances of its occurrence (what triggers off the misbehavior, at whom it is usually directed, what happens after it occurs). This information may aid you in understanding the root causes and/or factors contributing to the disturbance.

LINKING

The goal of the linking procedure is to seek a more harmonious balance in a child's life between the opposing forces of freedom and responsibility, and pleasure and pain. By using the following five linking procedures, you should obtain greater harmony between your needs and the needs of your child.

1. *Link Each Parental Restriction with a Freedom.* When you say no to a child, you are usually saying yes to something else. Make this explicit when you set limits by stating some of the acceptable options open to the child. For example, you might say, "Jim, you can't use the car on nights before school, but you can use it on Friday or Saturday nights."
2. *Link Each Liberty with a Responsibility.* To teach your child that with increased freedom comes added responsibility, you might say, "Bill, since you're going to be using the family car for your own needs now, you must begin to take some responsibility for the maintenance and care of the car. From now on, washing it will be up to you, and when you start making money from your part time job, I'll expect you to buy gas for the car on occasion."
3. *Link an Adolescent's Desires to His Earning Capacity.* At times, some of the desired expenditures of an adolescent go beyond the earning capacity of the family. It seems reasonable to link some of the financial desires of an adolescent to his capacity to meet part of the expenses. In this way you avoid turning the

child down completely. You might say, "If you want your own private phone, I'll pay for the installation charge if you pay for the monthly maintenance fee."

4. *Link Each Criticism with a Compliment.* When you soften a criticism with a compliment, children resent it less, e.g., "Hey, you're a real good-looking guy and I can't figure out why you don't take better care of your clothes and appearance."

5. *Link Each Punishment with Support and Reward.* When a child has been punished, he or she is in particular need of some understanding and comforting. Unfortunately, most parents tend to combine punishment with emotional distance and coldness towards the child. When punishing children, show them that they are still loveable by listening sympathetically to the pain they are suffering, and offer them both verbal and non-verbal signs of affection.

Also, when you punish a misbehavior, link it with a reward for a positive, incompatible behavior. An example of this combined "carrot and stick" approach is to penalize selfish behavior while praising altruistic acts. The carrot and stick approach has been found to result in very quick behavior change in a child.

ADDITIONAL READING

Chapman, A.H. *Management of Emotional Problems of Children and Adolescents.* Lippincott, Philadelphia, 1965. Further details on the linking procedure.

CRITICIZE CONSTRUCTIVELY

Criticism, as it was first instituted by Aristotle, was meant as a standard of judging well.

Johnson

In this chapter, ways of criticizing a child's behavior when it is not directly causing you a problem are discussed. Another technique — confronting — presents a method of handling personal problems with a child.

Constructive or positive criticism is educational in nature and attempts to focus a child's attention on the task by pointing out in a specific way what needs to be done or what went wrong; negative criticism, on the other hand, is judgmental in nature and is directed towards assigning blame or finding fault with a child's personality. Constructive criticism is an indirect method of calling attention to a child's mistakes by first finding something good in his behavior and then describing what went wrong and/or suggesting ways for improvement. To illustrate:

Negative criticism: "John, you're doing it all wrong!"
Constructive criticism: "John, you've got the spoons in the right place and you just need to reverse the knives and forks."

Negative criticism: "Anne, what's the matter with you, you failed math!"
Constructive criticism: "Anne, I see by your report card that you did well in Reading and Social Studies but that you are having difficulty with math. I know you've been trying hard, so we'll just have to get you a little extra help with this, don't you think?"

Negative criticism: "Marie, stop talking and get to work!"
Constructive criticism: "Marie, you will not finish your reading if you continue to talk."

Negative criticism: "Oh, you clumsy child. You did it again!"
Constructive criticism: "I see the milk is spilled. Here's a sponge to mop it up."

Negative criticism: "You have no friends. It's probably because you tease a lot."
Constructive criticism: "I think you'd be better liked if you said more nice things to others."

Discussion

Research has indicated that criticism is most effective when it is task-focused rather than approval-focused. In approval-focused criticism, you direct your disapproval towards the child, e.g., "Jane, I don't like children who talk without permission." In task-focused criticism, you direct your negative comments towards the activity of the child, e.g., "Jane, you will not finish your homework if you continue to talk." When you give approval-focused criticism, children tend to draw the inference that they have negative personality traits. It has also been found that children dislike or attribute less skill to teachers who criticize in an approval-focused fashion.

Criticism is always hard to take because no matter how tactfully presented it's by definition news that someone is dissatisfied with what you have done. It is best received, then, when it is given within a climate of acceptance and is sandwiched between words of appreciation. It is always easier to listen to unpleasant things after we have heard some praise for our good points. So try to point to something OK in the child's work or in the effort before offering criticism. For example, you might say:

"Boy, you worked hard to wipe this table clean. All that needs to be done now is removal of these small spots here."

Or, "You need help in figuring out division problems. All the rest of your answers are right!"

Some children have been corrected or criticized so much that when someone compliments them they can't believe or accept it. They think, "If they really knew me, they wouldn't be saying those nice things." Parents should try, then, to help children avoid such a "red-pencil mentality" by giving much more approval than disapproval or criticism. The following letter from a parent was printed in the *Rhode Island Churchman;* it all too accurately illustrates how prone we are to overdo criticism and "be at" children all the time rather than using moderation.

SATURDAY WITH A TEENAGE DAUGHTER

Are you going to sleep all day?. . .Who said you could use my hair spray?. . .Clean the dishes off the table. . . .Turn down that radio. . . . Have you made your bed?. . .That skirt is too short. . .Your closet is a mess. . . .Stand up straight. . . .Somebody has to go to the store. . . .Quit chewing your gum like that. . . .Your hair is too bushy. . . .I don't care if everybody else does have one. . . .Turn down that radio. . . .Have you done your homework?. . .Don't slouch. . . .You didn't make your bed. . . .Quit banging on the piano. . . .Why don't you iron it yourself?. . .Your fingernails are too long. . . .Look it up in the dictionary. . . .Sit up straight. . . .

Get off that phone. . . .Why did you ever buy that record?. . .Take the dog out. . . .You forgot to dust that table. . . .You've been in the bathroom long enough. . . .Turn off that radio and go to sleep."

Another day gone and not once did I say, "I love you." Dear Lord, forgive me.

Anonymous

PROMOTE SPECIAL COMPETENCE

Competency training involves teaching children to practice and acquire skills that are necessary for coping effectively with daily problems and opportunities. In addition to being generally competent, every child likes to feel that he or she has a special area of competence or expertise. This means that the child knows more about a particular topic than anyone else in the family, e.g., rocks and minerals, or that the child can do something better than the rest of the family, e.g., ski, converse, or play tennis. Such an area of distinction is ego-enhancing and provides a continuous source of nourishment to a child's self-esteem. No matter how far removed a child's expertise is from your own areas of interest, you should treat it with interest, respect, and admiration.

Parents can contribute to the development of a special competence by their encouragement and interest, and by providing the child with the required materials and training. Among the variety of hobbies that you might try to interest your child in are: collecting, model building, sewing-knitting, reading, photography, drawing-painting, and magic-tricks. Although there is considerable mess and clutter involved in some hobbies, there is also tremendous satisfaction to be gained by the real enthusiasts. Between the ages of 8–12, you will find that children will blow hot and cold for many different hobbies. By age 12, however, a child may settle on the one that he will stick with for the rest of his life. If your child shows no interest in a hobby despite the fact that he is often bored in his free time, try to share your own special interests and expose him to people who are real hobby enthusiasts. You might also take him to hobby shows and hobby shops.

Discussion

Hobbies or special areas of competence seem particularly important for children who lack the normal advantages of life, e.g., the middle child, the physically handicapped or unattractive child, the socially-isolated child, and the underachieving child. According to Alfred Adler, the late psychoanalyst, we are all born with an innate sense of inferiority which is felt as an inner feeling of inadequacy and a need to demonstrate to oneself and others that we are capable and able to master the environment. Children with special problems or handicaps especially feel the need to be competent.

GIVE AN ALLOWANCE

Research has indicated that children who engage in petty thievery, i.e., take the property of others, tend to have been brought up in a home environment where their parents either ignored their financial needs or gave them large sums of money to spend.

By providing a regular, modest allowance to children parents achieve a threefold purpose: they recognize the legitimate financial needs of children; they promote a sense of responsibility and decision-making; and they teach the value of money. An allowance is not a bribe but an opportunity to give realistic, first-hand experience in planning how money is to be spent and how to get value for it. Most child development experts agree on the value of a regular allowance.

Allowance typically begins at age five or six. The best method is to give the same amount on the same day of the week so that the child will know exactly what to expect. With a very young child, you may want to give him half the allowance, twice a week. Each family must decide for themselves how much allowance to give a child, based on such factors as family status, usual practices in the community, and what specific purchases the item is to cover. Apart from incidental treats, the cost of transportation, school supplies, and hobby materials must come out of some allowances.

In Chevy Chase, Maryland, a particularly affluent suburb, school age children receive an average weekly allowance of $1.80. The older the child is, of course, the greater his monetary needs will be. For a mature teenager who must use his allowance for dating and clothing expenses, a sum of $20 to $25 a week might not be excessive. Extra money might also be available for special labor around the house, but allowances should never be tied to chores or be disallowed as a punishment. A 1972 survey by *Money* magazine revealed a median allowance of 25¢ for children under seven, 50¢ for 8–9 year olds, a dollar for 10–13 year olds, and $2.50 for 14 and 15 year olds. However, the range was wide, depending on regional price differentials and cultures.

General Guidelines

1. Expect children to make mistakes and buy unwisely at first. Let them make mistakes and learn from them.
2. Don't *insist* the child save something from the allowance. Let the child decide how to spend it.
3. Don't withhold the allowance as a punishment.
4. Don't link an allowance with household chores, or else you may raise a child who won't lift a finger except for pay.
5. Make an allowance large enough to cover reasonable expenses, and keep the child's expanding needs in mind in determining the size of the allowance.
6. Begin a weekly allowance sometime around the child's fifth birthday, or when daily requests for candy and ice cream appear.
7. You may give advice on how to spend the money and set a good example yourself of wise buying, but don't criticize a child's spending errors constantly.
8. Encourage children to earn extra money on their own so they can see the relationship between effort and money.
9. Do not make the child feel indebted to you for the allowance. Children should see it as their just share of the family income.
10. High school students should be able to manage money on a monthly basis.

Discussion

Apart from allowances, another useful technique for developing money management skills in children is a personal savings account.

Thus, parents should encourage their children to plan ahead for future financial needs by saving some of the money they receive from allowances, gifts, and odd jobs.

ADDITIONAL READING

Weinstein, G.W. *Children and Money: A Guide for Parents.* Schocken Books. New York, 1976.

ASSIGN CHORES

Man must work. That is certain as the sun. But he may work grudgingly or he may work gratefully; he may work as a man, or he may work as a machine. There is no work so rude, that he may not exalt it; no work so impassive, that he may not breathe a soul into it; no work so dull that he may not enliven it.

Henry Giles

The assignment of chores to children has a twofold purpose: to teach them the concept of family sharing and to introduce them to the world of work. Work has enormous meaning for the development of a sense of competence and self-esteem. Some of the skills you learn from good work habits are: concentration, persistence, concern for quality and accuracy, how to make judgments and decisions, and the ability to follow through on one's own without supervision.

What can you expect from your children in regard to work? As any kindergarten teacher will tell you, preschool children are capable of setting the dinner table, vacuuming a room, and making their bed. By ages 11-12, they can take out the trash, go to the store, mow the lawn, etc. According to a recent government survey, parents report that 65% of six-year-old children do some chores at home, and the average amount of time they spend on chores a day is 30 minutes. By age 11, 90% of the children living at home do chores and spend 50 minutes per day completing them. Girls tend to spend a few minutes longer a day on chores than boys. The survey also noted that three out of four children aged 6–11 had one regular home task or more. Moreover, the proportion of children doing 3 or more tasks regularly more than doubled over this age range, increasing from 20% at age 6 to 47% among 11 year olds.

Most children do not like doing chores, and the most common ploy they use to avoid chores is to plead, "I'm too busy." The best response to this is to remind the child that chores take priority over other activities during certain periods of the day. You will also find that children do not like to be assigned chores that isolate them from the rest of the family, e.g., cleaning the cellar. In addition, children accept chores more willingly when their parents work alongside them such as when a parent and child clean a room together.

Guidelines

1. To build a child's pride in his work, give praise and recognition for a chore well done.
2. Provide a wide variety of chores to do and let the children rotate these tasks at stated intervals and have a voice in the assignment of tasks.
3. Perform your share of chores cheerfully and take *pride* in your work. Take turns doing the most menial tasks with your children. The most important influence on a child will be your example. Be a model of cheerfully accepting work responsibility, being prompt and efficient in performance of the task, and showing a spirit of cooperation and sharing the work load.
4. Give children some high prestige, interesting jobs, e.g., cooking the evening meal, household repairing, or constructing bookshelves, even though you will have to spend considerable time and energy teaching them how to perform these complex, challenging tasks. To grow in self-esteem and competency, teenagers in particular, need these advanced learning opportunities.
5. Endeavor to make work as enjoyable as possible but don't try to make all chores easy or fun. Kids need to learn that work, even though meaningful, will not always be pleasant.
6. Be sure to schedule chores so that they do not interfere with a child's needs for: free play time, study time, family interaction time, or rest-relaxation time.

7. Give a child guidance and supervision on a chore but allow considerable freedom in working out the details for himself. In offering feedback on a child's performance, take the middle ground between setting unrealistically high standards and tolerating slipshod work. Offer constructive criticism which points out the positive aspects of the performance while showing the way to further improvement.

8. Be aware of children's passive-resistent tactics to work, e.g., delay, arguments, deliberate ineptitude, and sulkiness.

9. Don't assign a chore as a way of punishing a child because this communicates that work is not a positive activity but a punitive one.

10. Explain to a child the reason the chore has to be done and why you are asking him to assume responsibility for it. Discuss with your child the importance of social responsibility — why and how it contributes to the comfort and well-being of all the family members, including himself.

11. If a child does extra work at home, you should endeavor to pay him for it. This will also involve you in supervising the extra work to be sure it is done reliably and conscientiously. It will provide the child with excellent training for future jobs outside the home where he will also be supervised and paid.

12. If you consider the chores you assign a child to be demeaning and disagreeable, your negative attitude will probably rub off on your child. Work attitudes are catching. Be sure your attitude is one of respect for the value of work and pride in a job well done — no matter how boring or menial the task!

Work is love made visible.

Kahlil Gibran

ALLOW SUPERVISED EXPERIMENTATION

When they are young, children should be given limited choices in decisions affecting them; when they are teenagers, parents should try to ensure that children make informed choices about important decisions, such as the use of drugs, sex, and so on. Rather than laying down do's and don'ts for teenagers, parents can help by providing them with information and experiences needed to make rational conclusions. The advantages as well as the dangers and pitfalls of cigarette and alcohol use should be pointed out in advance to prepare the children for it.

It also seems advisable to have children initially experience smoking and drinking under parental supervision. When parents forbid their children to experience certain behaviors that are potentially harmful, e.g., drinking, smoking, this prohibition often results in the taboo behaviors becoming more appealing to the children so that they are more likely to engage in these behaviors outside the home. It seems wiser, then, for parents to provide a home environment where children can sample these potentially harmful behaviors under careful supervision. In this way, having experienced drinking and smoking under parental guidance, and having learned the facts about the pro's and con's of frequent usage of alcohol and cigarettes from his parents, a child will be in a better position to make an informed decision about his future use of both items.

A one-sided training is to point out the dangers of a behavior and to forbid the child ever to engage in the behavior, e.g., puff a cigarette sip wine, or light a match. Two-sided training involves describing honestly both the advantages and disadvantages of potentially harmful behaviors. One-sided propaganda — the telling of a one-sided story — has been found to be more vulnerable to counterpropaganda than telling both sides of a story. After you have described the good and bad aspects of a behavior, you can further help by having the child experience the behavior under your guidance. Children who have held a match under supervision and have felt the heat are less likely to light matches when they are alone than children who have had no direct experience with matches.

Discussion

Supervised experimentation can be considered a form of innoculation. A person is typically made resistant to some attacking virus if he has had a previous exposure to a weakened dose of the virus. A mild dose stimulates your defenses so that you are in a better position to overcome any massive attack to which you may later be exposed. Having had some experience with alcoholic beverages at home, a child should be in a better position to handle the consumption of liquor when he is on his own.

GIVE FREEDOM TO FAIL

He only is exempt from failure who makes no efforts.

Whately

Many adults find it difficult to let mistakes happen. The incident of spilt milk or the fight on the playground should be welcomed as teachable moments which can help your children learn from living. As a preventive measure against your child developing anxiety or fear of failure, you should treat mistakes and errors as a normal, expected part of the learning process. By discussing what went wrong, you point the way to future successes.

Allowing a learning leeway means that you expect a child to make mistakes when he is learning a new skill, e.g., learning table manners or how to read, spell, or ride a bike. Be patient, a child has so much to learn and everything takes practice!

A parent's attitude towards errors and failure will contribute to the psychological learning climate in the home. A calm, understanding, uncritical attitude towards mistakes will create a climate of safety and security. Too much insistence on perfection can give children a fear of making mistakes. Every child should grow up feeling it's not a tragedy, not a catastrophe, to make a mistake.

Discussion

Underlying this approach is a conviction that mistakes are a necessary part of learning. Children learn, in large measure, through trial-and-error discovery. So rather than stressing rote learning through adult directives, it seems best to provide varied opportunities for self-learning. For example, you might let a toddler place different size rings on a spindle in the wrong sequence. Then you would ask if it looks right to him, i.e., encourage task analysis by the child.

Part II
Ways to Build Positive
Family Relationships

INTRODUCTION

Friendships are fragile things, and require as much care in handling as any other fragile and precious thing.

Randolph S. Bourne

Studies have shown that the disciplinary practices described in the first part of this book are most effective when applied within the context of a close parent-child relationship. It seems that children learn discipline best when they feel that their parents love, understand, and respect them. An open communication between parents and children is essential for real understanding and closeness to develop. Relationships do not just happen, they are the results of much diligence, hard work, and self-sacrifice. A description of the various components of a positive family relationship will be presented in this part of the book. The basic assumption of this book is that the optimal parent-child relationship is not one of master-slave, but a friendship relationship based on equality, respect, common interests, and caring. You cannot purchase a child's friendship by making a child feel indebted to you because of your sacrifices of money or time; you have to earn children's friendships by being a friend — this means mutual loving, liking, understanding, and spending many enjoyable times together.

As Edward Zigler, Professor of Psychology at Yale University recently said: "There is a magic that rests in the relationship between a child and a warm, sensitive, and knowledgeable adult. It is in the fullness of that relationship that we see the child's path to growth and development." The goal of this part of the book is to sketch, in rough outline, some facets of this magic relationship that we all seek with our children.

HOW TO LISTEN SO CHILDREN WILL TALK

A good listener is not only popular everywhere, but after a while he gets to know something.

Wilson Mizner

Listening is an active process of hearing and trying to understand the message underlying a child's words. A major complaint family members make of one another is, "No one really listens to me." Children in particular feel this way because most communication in the home is a one-way street — from parent to child. To assess whether or not you are a good listener, consider the following questions. Do you make sure to give your child your undivided attention when you listen? Are you so convinced of your own importance that you can't wait to interrupt a child or find an opening to start talking? Do you tend to monopolize the conversation by lecturing, preaching, reassuring, etc., or do you have a real dialogue with children? Do you not only have frequent talks with your children, but do you have in-depth talks in which there is a mutual sharing of feelings, beliefs, conflicts, doubts, values, and dreams? The following guidelines are offered to assist you in reviewing the listening process.

Guidelines on How to Listen to Children

1. *Be Interested.* If you show a sincere interest in children and their activities you will not only get them to open up, but you will make them feel important. Also, children tend to feel very close to an adult who, by expressing concern and caring, gets them talking about themselves.

2. *Be Available.* There seem to be certain critical periods in a child's life when he or she needs a parent to be there to listen. When they experience internal emotion because of a crisis, trauma, or disappointment in life, children particularly need a parent to be available to listen and supply whatever comfort or support is needed. Children also need to feel that their parents are readily available to share good news or joyful experiences. Children must feel that you are not too busy to talk or that other priorities come first.

The period right after school seems to be an especially important time to be available to a child. If both parents work, then one parent should reserve this time to be available to talk with the child on the phone. A substitute parent, e.g., mother's helper, should also be available to a child at this time. In this connection, a growing problem in our society is the increasing number of "latch key" children, i.e., kids who come home from school to an empty house. Such children are particularly prone to a variety of problems (school, drug, and behavior).

Another period when children seem to keenly feel parent unavailability is when a parent is on the phone. I know of one father who solved this problem by devising a signal that the children could use when he was on the phone to indicate that they really needed him. At these times they were to come up to the father with both hands on their heads! This unusual procedure worked very well because it allowed everybody's needs to be met.

A study* of well adjusted college men revealed that such men reported a high degree of father availability as well as father nurturance. So it seems that being available to children is an important aspect of fathering as well as mothering.

3. *Give Undivided Attention.* To be a good listener you must give your complete attention and concentration. Select a quiet spot and an unhurried time of the day to listen. Don't try to iron, cook, or watch TV when you really want to listen. Forget about the telephone and other distractions. Maintain eye contact to show that you are really with the child. Provide daily opportunities for the child to be completely alone with you even if only for a few minutes; you might say, "Let's go for a little walk together." or "Let's go to the den for a private time."

4. *Be Patient and Encourage Talking.* Some children need an explicit invitation to start talking, e.g., "Tell me about your day." or "I'd like to hear about what happened in school today." To keep a child talking, you might use such minimal

*Biller, Henry. *Father, Child, and Sex Role: Paternal Determinants of Personality Development.* Heath Lexington Books, Lexington, Massachusetts, 1971.

encouragers as "Hmmm," "Un-Hm," and "I see." You might also ask brief open-ended questions to further draw a child out, e.g., "And then what happened?" or "What did you do to get him so upset?"

Avoid cutting children off before they have finished speaking, e.g., saying "Yes, but . . . ." Most parents do this a lot, perhaps because they think they know what a child is going to say. Rather, when children come to you emotionally upset by something, you can help them calm down by patiently asking for a detailed description of what happened — all the specifics, including exactly what triggered off the upset and what the child thinks and feels about the whole thing.

When children dwell on a problem situation and describe it in the fullest possible detail, it becomes clarified in their minds so that they are able to find solutions to it by themselves. Even when you do find it necessary to offer suggestions for resolving the problem, your recommendations assume greater significance and meaning to the child if they are preceded by such verbal reflections about the event.

5. *Watch Your Body Language.* Body language refers to the non-verbal ways in which we send messages to children. Many adults still do not know how to use their bodies to give a child the message, "I'm listening, I'm interested, and I'm paying attention." There are six major signs a person gives when paying attention to another: faces the other squarely, sits close to the other (about 3–4 feet away), maintains an alert, erect body posture, leans toward the other, makes eye contact, and tries to be at home or relaxed. You should also avoid nervous mannerisms and try to show an interested, friendly facial expression and tone of voice.

6. *Be Empathic.* Perhaps the most important skill of a good listener is the ability to be empathic, that is, the ability to put yourself in someone else's shoes and to imagine what they are experiencing apart from your own thoughts and feelings about the matter. It's the skill of feeling the emotional vibrations of a child and communicating this understanding to the child.

7. *Help Clarify and Relate Experiences.* Listening is an active process in which you attempt to provide a child with a deeper

understanding of inner thoughts and feelings. In active listening you try to clarify a child's expressions by paraphrasing them or stating them in your own words. In paraphrasing, you use your wider vocabulary to help children express themselves as accurately and clearly as possible. Sometimes an apt phrase will bring a feeling into clearer focus: Child: I got so upset I didn't know what I was doing. Parent: You mean you panicked. Apart from assisting in clearer communication by paraphrasing, you should help children build bridges between their experiences, feelings, and behavior. For instance, you might help a child connect her recent feelings of anxiety and sleeplessness to upcoming exams in school. A good listener will also attempt to draw justifiable inferences, conclusions, and generalizations; summarize what has been said; make comparisons by using similies and metaphors; and continually check with the child to verify the accuracy of all understandings.

8. *Reflect Feelings.* A particularly effective listening technique is to be a mirror to your child's feelings by verbally reflecting them back to him so the emotions can be better accepted, expressed, and understood. Young children, especially, are not tuned in to their feelings, nor can they express them as well as adults. Thus, you might reflect a child's feelings by commenting, "It sounds like you're very angry at your math teacher for not listening to your side of the story."

Reflection of feelings means encouraging children to share their feelings at that moment and to explore them verbally. It is particularly useful when children are experiencing powerful emotions (positive or negative) which they may or may not be fully aware of. It involves restating or rephrasing what the child has just said: Child: School is dumb! I hate it! Parent: Sounds like you're pretty angry at something that happened today in school. Young children need to learn that it is OK to have angry feelings but it is not OK to act on them. In this regard you might say, "I know you're mad at her for breaking your toy and you feel like hitting her, but say it with words, don't hit."

When you avoid evaluating or putting down a child's feelings and accept them as normal and legitimate, you help him to accept rather than disown them. After negative feelings are accepted and expressed, they tend to lose their intensity, which opens the way for more positive emotions and constructive solutions.

It is difficult for most adults to accept the strong negative feelings of children (anger, sadness) since we were not raised that way and strong emotions tend to upset us. Consequently, we have to make a conscious effort to reflect feelings back to children and see if this technique is helpful.

9. *Avoid Roadblocks.* Most of the time parents talk *at* children rather than *with* them. Instead of listening to children by paraphrasing or reflecting feelings, parents tend to respond to children in a way that blocks or inhibits further communication by the child. Ways to throw up roadblocks to a child's further talking about a problem include: giving orders ("Don't talk to me in that tone of voice!"), belittling the child ("That's silly."), being reassuring ("You'll get over it."), name calling ("Only babies cry."), lecturing ("The reason you feel this way is . . . . "), evaluating ("What a terrible thing to do."), denying ("You can't still be mad."), or giving solutions ("This is what you have to do about it."). The net effect of these roadblocks is to close off further communications by the child and/or to show lack of respect for the child. Children soon learn not to come to you with their problems when you throw up such barriers.

10. *Listen to Nonverbal Messages.* Most of the messages children send are communicated nonverbally, i.e., by their tone of voice, the look on their faces, their energy level, body posture, or change in behavior patterns (child suddenly does not give the customary hello when returning home). You can often learn more from the way a child says something than from what is said. Thus, when a child comes in obviously upset (slams the doors, goes straight to his room to be alone), be sure to find a quiet time later in the day when he has his emotions under greater control to encourage him to explore his feelings. You might say, for example, "Did anything happen in school today?" or "You seem very upset about something."

LISTENING WITH THE THIRD EAR

Listening with the third ear refers to the skill of comprehending the subtle, tiny clues children give to their hidden thoughts and feelings. It is comparable to the skill of reading between the lines of a letter for what is left unsaid. It means being sensitive to the "bad vibrations" a child sends out when he is emotionally upset. Often when children most desire their parents to hear them they only whisper their need. This whisper will be inaudible to parents who are not tuned in to inconspicuous signals.

If you feel your third ear or sixth sense is not operative, try attending to small signs that a child is behaving unusually. For example, you should be alert to abnormal peculiarities in care of clothing (unkept?), tone of voice, facial expression, energy level, movements and posture, breathing (fast-slow?), physical distance to you (at your side constantly or always far away?), sudden hostility towards small children or pets (Is this really meant for you?), or proneness to daydreams.

Apart from a sensitivity to nonverbal patterns of behaviors in a child, listening with the third ear involves listening "between the lines" when a child talks. Ask yourself what is the child trying to tell me. You might need to ask probing questions to discern or clarify the child's intentions or underlying emotions.

Parents should also be particularly sensitive to the absence of usual behavior for this will often give valuable clues to a child's inner feelings. An obvious example is when a child does not eat, sleep, play, or concentrate as well as usual. A more subtle example is the failure of a child to give the customary goodnight kiss or welcome home smile.

An examination of the content of a child's drawings and reported dreams will often give clues to a child's unconscious feelings.

Once these clues have been noted, you should try to conjecture or intuitively feel what they reflect about the inner emotional state of the child. Most parents gained considerable experience doing this when they attempted to figure out why their baby was crying when he clearly was not hungry or wet.

Listening with the third ear means attending to miniscule clues left by your child, as well as to your inner feelings and intuitions about your child. It means knowing how your child feels without his saying.

The need to listen carefully to what children are not saying is highlighted in the following poem:

THE REAL ME

Don't be fooled by me. Don't be fooled by the face I wear.
For I wear a thousand masks and none of them are me.
I give the impression that I'm secure, that all is sunny and
    unruffled with me, within as well as without.
That confidence is my name and coolness my game,
That the water's calm and I'm in command.
But don't believe me. Please.
Beneath dwells the real me in confusion, in fear, and aloneness.
But I hide this. I don't want anybody to know it.
I panic at the thought of my weakness and fear of being exposed.
That's why I frantically create a mask to hide behind,
To help me pretend, to shield me from the glance that knows.
But such a glance is precisely my salvation. My only salva-
    tion. And I know it.
That is if it's followed by acceptance, if it's followed by love.
But I don't tell you this. I don't dare. I'm afraid to.
I'm afraid that your glance will not be followed by acceptance
    and love.
And so begins the parade of masks. And my life becomes a front.
I idly chatter to you in the suave tones of surface talk.
I tell you everything that is really nothing and nothing of
    what's everything.
Of what's crying within me;
So when I'm going through my routine do not be fooled.
Please listen carefully and try to hear what I'm not saying.
I dislike hiding. Honestly!
I'd really like to be genuine and spontaneous, and me, but you've
    got to help me.
You've got to hold out your hand, even when that's the last
    thing I seem to want.
Each time you're kind and gentle, and encouraging, my heart
    begins to grow wings, very small wings, very feeble wings.

With your sensitivity and sympathy and your power of understand-
ing you can breathe life into me. I want you to know that.
I want you to know how important you are to me, how you can be
the creator of the person that is me if you choose to.
Please choose me. You alone can break down the wall behind
which
I tremble, you alone can remove my mask.
Please . . . do not pass me by.
It will not be easy for you.
I fight against the very thing I cry out for, but I am told
that love is stronger than walls, and in this lies my hope.
Please try to beat down those walls with firm hands, but with
gentle hands – for a child is very sensitive.
Who am I, you may wonder. I am someone you know very well.
For I am every man you meet and I am every woman you meet.

ANON.

HOW TO TALK
SO CHILDREN WILL LISTEN

Daily experiences will result in greater learning for children if they
have regular opportunities to share them with you, discuss them, and
examine their implications. So be sure your priorities are such that
you have scheduled time each day to have informal discussions with
your children. Avoid laying down the law or insisting upon agreement in these discussions lest they become arguments. They should
be free discussions in which various points of view are expressed and
everyone both talks and listens. Not only will these discussions
promote close bonds between you and your child, but you will find
that they are one of the most powerful character building skills you
possess.

Discussions should be characterized by an open exchange of ideas,
a mutual sharing of experiences, a demonstration of honesty, a dialogue of mutual respect, and a willingness to learn on your part.
Ideally, the discussions should be a continuous, ongoing procedure in
your home, not an infrequent occurrence. Topics for discussion
should be as wide ranging as one's daily experiences, including
hobbies, sports, school, personal difficulties, current events, etc. In

the two previous sections, the art of listening to children was discussed. Since the ability to talk to children is just as important for a good discussion, the following guidelines are offered to assist you in improving this skill:

Guidelines on How to Talk so Children Will Listen

1. *Be Brief.* Adults tend to do most of the talking when conversing with children. Be brief and succinct. Avoid dominating the conversation by lengthy monologues or sermons. Give equal time for the child to talk. Listen as much as you talk. Seek reciprocal rather than one-sided communication, i.e., a dialogue rather than monologue.
2. *Use Simple, Concrete Words.* Use short, simple words that are in the child's vocabulary. Make frequent use of his own words and expressions.

   Also try to express yourself concretely and specifically rather than being general or vague. Kids are visually minded — they see and understand pictures better than abstract concepts. Thus, when explaining something to a child it is best to make your point by vividly painting a picture with words. This is done by using plenty of concrete examples that draw upon their experiences. For example, you might relate the abstract concept death to something the child has directly experienced ("like when your dog Tora died, he didn't move."). Also, make frequent use of figurative language (simile, metaphor, symbol) which stirs a child's imagination. It is a picturesque, vivid, and colorful form of expression that appeals directly to their emotions, e.g., The boy felt lonely, like a football lying on a basketball court.
3. *Be Respectful.* Talk with a child and not at him. Don't be patronizing, dogmatic, or talk down to a child. Be courteous and polite, e.g., don't interrupt when the child is speaking. Consider what you are going to say in advance so you can say it in the clearest possible way while taking into account the child's feelings. How you say things is more important than what you say, so maintain a friendly, respectful tone of voice and non-bossy manner.

4. *Be Animated.* Conversations with children should be lively, vigorous, brisk, and spirited. Like an animated cartoon they should move right along. Avoid long pauses or deep reflections before responding. Don't speak with an expressionless, "stone" face, or talk in a dull, monotonous tone of voice.

5. *Be Direct.* Be honest and give a straight answer to a child's question. Also be *congruent* in your expressions which means saying what you genuinely mean and feel inside at that moment. If you're feeling annoyed at a child's behavior, express this feeling directly rather than taking it out on the child in other ways. The child probably already knows you are annoyed. Children find it easier to understand your messages when you are straight with them.

6. *Self-Disclose.* To come across as a real person to your child means revealing some of your personal needs, weaknesses, dreams, and emotions. Have you ever talked to your child, for example, about what makes you afraid or what makes you particularly happy? A deliberate disclosure of your private thoughts and feelings will lead to greater trust and closeness with your child.

   Research has shown that in social interactions between two people, self-disclosure by one person tends to be reciprocated by the other person. In other words, the more you reveal your needs, weaknesses, and dreams to a child, the more he will disclose similar aspects of his private world to you. Consequently, the less likely it will be that you will live as two strangers in the same house!

7. *Enjoy Talking to Children.* If you really enjoy talking to a child, chances are that he will enjoy speaking to you. Enjoyment of children is based upon a sincere interest in them and their reactions to life. A sense of humor is also helpful. A sign of real enjoyment of children is that you are friendly, pleasant and relaxed when conversing with them. Being pleasant means having a positive outlook toward life, i.e., cheerful and optimistic and not 'critical, complaining, or pessimistic. Have fun talking to your children and getting them to talk to you. If you have fun, they will too, and it will be equally rewarding to you all.

8. *Be Relevant.* Stay on the topic of conversation. Don't try to control or lead the conversation around to your hidden agenda or pet topics. Let the direction of the discussion flow naturally. Try to talk about what interests the child at that moment.

9. *Select the Right Time.* Don't try to have a discussion when someone is hurried, tense, upset, or tired. Find a time when you are both in the mood to talk and you can give the child your undivided attention. This means you're not busy cooking, watching TV, or writing letters while you're trying to talk. A good time to talk would be right after school when the child is having a snack.

10. *Avoid Arguments.* If parents and children can respectfully disagree and avoid raising their voices, then they can probably avoid letting a discussion deteriorate into an argument. Remember that the goal of a discussion is companionship not one-upmanship; pleasantness, not animosity. Try to avoid sensitive topics which either you or the child cannot discuss calmly. Be alert to the early warning signs of emotional upset in either party and quickly change the topic of conversation when the signs are present. Hopefully there will not be too many touchy topics between you and your children and you will be able to freely discuss differing values and such taboo topics as death, religion, sex, money, and growing old.

Discussion

According to Haim Ginott, the main reason that few real dialogues exist between parents and children is because kids resent being preached to, talked at, and criticized. Ginott maintains that conversations between adults and children typically sound like two monologues, one consisting of criticism and instructions, the other of denials and pleadings. The tragedy of such interactions, he states, lies not in the lack of love but in the lack of parental respect; not in the lack of intelligence, but in the lack of a parental communication skill.

CELEBRATE WITH RITUALS AND CEREMONIES

Family *rituals* are regular events which are observed at certain times, in accord with prescribed rules. Each family develops its own rituals as it develops its own identity and pride. Family rituals generate feelings of togetherness, joy, and a sense of belonging. They represent a unique way for a family to be together and make their mutual life different from every other family. Rituals enhance a group relationship and make it special and private at times.

It is helpful to establish many rituals in the home. In addition to traditional holiday observances, many families have added their own special rituals, such as a family day on Sunday which features a festive meal and entertainment by talented family members on special occasions. Other activities which can be made rituals include storytelling, reading poetry, arts and crafts activities, preparing special foods, family sports events, and family talk time at the end of the day.

Ceremonies

Apart from rituals, ceremonies honoring family members can be used to add zest and enthusiasm to family living.

A ceremony is an interesting, exciting event that makes a child the center of attention. It can be used to reward children, or show approval, or caring.

The use of ceremonies as a technique for motivating children to achieve or perform desirable behaviors has held a prominent place in many character-building projects, e.g., girl and boy scouts. Moreover, churches have long used rites and ceremonies to inspire awe and reverence, as well as to celebrate or commemorate special occasions.

Parents should make regular use of ceremonies to give their children added incentive to achieve, e.g., recognize a child's intellectual, emotional, or social achievement by a special cake, trophy, speech, party, or family gathering. Ceremonies can also be used to express general love and caring for a child, e.g., a "nonbirthday" party.

They can also serve to give public notice of a child's "rite of passage" into a more advanced developmental level, e.g., becoming a man or a woman (puberty or reaching the voting age). The purpose of such public rituals is not only to foster pride by publicly recognizing and celebrating the event, but also to notify all concerned to expect more mature behavior from the child.

Ceremonies make an event memorable by their novelty, the intensity of emotion, and the feeling of family sharing and camaraderie. They relieve boredom by adding change and festivity to family life.

SHOWING EMPATHY

Instead of putting others in their places, put yourself in their place.
Baptist Trumpet

Empathy means trying, as accurately and sensitively as you can, to show children that you understand them from their point of view. It means imaginatively getting inside children and looking at the world through their perspective and feeling what this is like. It also involves communicating to children this understanding of their inner experience. Empathy means feeling with a child rather than feeling for (sympathy). Seeing things from a child's internal framework results in your beginning to experience the events of a child's life as if they were your own. This "as if" quality is similar to reading a novel and being drawn out of yourself so that you actually live with the main characters by feeling some of their feelings and thinking some of their thoughts. Like a tuning fork, you emotionally vibrate in accord with the feelings of the characters.

For example, if your son just came in and stated that he just hit his first home run in a little league game, you might empathically say: "Wow, you must be bursting with joy. It must feel great to accomplish what you've been hoping for!" In other words, you use your own past experiences and hunches to guess what a child must be feeling and you phrase your response so the child knows you clearly understand these feelings. Thus, if your daughter just mentioned that she was shamed by the teacher in front of the whole class you might say, "It must have hurt your feelings." or "You must have hated the teacher at that moment." or "It must have been terribly embarassing!" It should be noted that the focus of these responses is not on the event *per se* but on describing the child's thoughts and feelings toward the emotionally-arousing event.

By using your powers of empathy, you can often get behind a child's defenses to understand the real meaning of a child's misbehavior. One parent reported, for instance, that the vicious bullying of an older child towards a younger sibling seemed to be the act of a heartless monster until she realized that the older child was acting meanly because he felt the mother favored the younger child. The only way the older child knew to express his feelings of rejection and jealousy was to lash out aggressively. The first step in resolving this problem was for the mother to coexperience the hurt thoughts and feelings of the older child and communicate this understanding to him. Nearly all problem children have as a part of their life history the fact that they have not been fully understood by those whom they wish or need to have know them best, i.e., their parents.

In punishing a child you can often soften the blow by showing empathy for the good motives or intentions underlying the misdeed. For example you might say, "You're yelling because you have strong feelings about this." or "I know you are late for dinner because you were having so much fun playing and it was hard to break away." or "You don't want to go to school because you're bored there and you get restless." Children tend to take criticism and punishment better after you have pointed out something good about them. When parents see the good intention behind an act, then children think that perhaps they are not so bad or abnormal as they might have thought. Rather, they will more likely think "Perhaps I don't have to judge myself so harshly."

Guidelines for Showing Empathy

1. Be as concrete and specific as you can in describing your understanding of the child. Avoid abstract or obtuse terms.
2. While being empathic, suspend your own judgments concerning the goodness or badness of a child's thoughts and feelings.

3. Listen with your "third ear" to the nonverbal cues the child is sending out concerning internal experiences.
4. Reflect the underlying thoughts and feelings rather than the surface content of what the child is saying.
5. Use observation, inference, and guess work to gain a reasonably accurate picture of the flow of thoughts and feelings inside the child. Then communicate this understanding so the child can correct any misperceptions.

Discussion

By listening empathically to the thoughts and feelings of a child, you not only promote self-understanding in that you encourage more accurate self-listening, but you develop self-acceptance since you validate the child's inner experience, i.e., you show it makes sense from another person's point of view. As long as our reactions seem reasonable to others, then we are less likely to feel strange, isolated, or confused, and fewer problems are likely to emerge since the child feels, "Well, at least my parents understand me."

Studies have shown that empathy is a reaction that we can seldom expect from our parents or even our friends. On the other hand, it is a skill that one can learn, and professional therapists and counselors rate it as the most important personal characteristic of a helping professional. Also noteworthy is the research finding that people who experience the strongest degree of empathic reactions towards others are the ones most willing to help others, even though it means jeopardizing their own welfare.

Finally, it is important to note that there are two basic types of understanding, only one of which is empathy. Nonempathic understanding means knowing *why* a child has misbehaved, rather than experiencing *what* it is the child is thinking and feeling at the time. Empathy, on the other hand, does not try to determine why a child is behaving in a certain way, but to understand the child from his or her point of view. Thus empathy may involve understanding how it may have seemed OK to the child to steal, and actually feeling the emptiness inside which motivated the act. Of course, it is particularly difficult to be empathic when we disagree or morally condemn the act of a child. Rather than being empathic, our first inclination when a child misbehaves is to impose our views and penalties on the child. After a child sees that you first understand the situation from his point of view, however, then the child will be better able to look at the situation from other perspectives and accept penalties.

Teaching Empathy

In addition to modeling understanding, you should take every opportunity to directly teach this reaction to children. One way to encourage your children to be empathic towards others is to point out to them the effect of their behavior on others — especially on the feelings of others. You might say, for example, "Pulling the cat's hair can hurt the cat and cause him pain." or "If you don't call your aunt and thank her for the present, she may think you are ungrateful and feel bad." or "I feel very annoyed and frustrated when you tie up the phone for hours."

As part of explaining the consequences of your child's acts on others, you should include a description of the needs, vulnerabilities, or desires of others, whenever it seems appropriate. Thus, you might say, "She's afraid of the water, so please don't splash her." or "I know he's very lonely and would appreciate a visit from you." A reflection by you about the possible motives underlying the behavior of others will also contribute towards the development of empathy in your child. You might say, for example, "I think that dog bit you because you frightened him by suddenly running at him."

Discussion

By developing children's capacity for empathy, you provide them with a powerful emotional and cognitive support for the development of moral controls. An empathic person is more likely to apply self-praise after helping another and self-condemnation after hurting someone. This internal locus of evaluation forms the basis for conscience development and self-discipline.

LOVING CHILDREN

The greatest happiness of life is the conviction that we are loved,
loved for ourselves, or rather loved in spite of ourselves.

Victor Hugo

Loving a child seems to have three essential components, namely, unconditional positive regard, cherishing, and caring. A brief description of each component is presented below.

Unconditional Positive Attitude

Unconditional love means that there are no strings attached to it. It's the kind of love that makes no conditions or stipulations, i.e., there is no saying I'll love you only if you do this or don't do that. Rather, the child feels, I am loved because I am. Unconditional positive love means that you will always regard your child as an intrinsically worthwhile and loveable person no matter what he does or fails to do. Practically speaking, this involves welcoming your child in your home despite such acts as: marrying someone of a different race or faith; becoming a drug addict or alcoholic; commiting a heinous crime; or denouncing you in public, *a la* Patty Hearst.

Signs of this special kind of existential love are parental expressions of: "I love you just because you're you."; "You're precious."; "You're really a special child to me." Another sign would be the absence of parental threats regarding loss of love, e.g., "I won't love you anymore if you continue to do that!" Children need to feel that there is at least one solid, dependable source of security in this world of rapid change and confused values, namely, the unwavering love of their parents. So be careful not to use withdrawal of love or rejection as a punishment for misbehavior. No matter how angry you are at a child's actions, the child should still feel secure in your basic love and acceptance.

In a close, unconditional relationship, both parent and child know each other well enough to be aware of one another's psychological and interpersonal weaknesses, but these weaknesses are accepted and not exploited. In such a relationship, the parties are free to be them-selves and act spontaneously without fear or worry of being rejected for what they do.

As opposed to unconditional love, there is love based on merit ("I'll love you because of what you have done") or expectations ("I'll love you because you have fulfilled my expectations, because you do your duty, because you are like me"). The negative aspect of this kind of love (some call it "fatherly" love) is that when one feels loved because you have earned it then there is always doubt and insecurity that the love will disappear one day because you may do something to displease the parent. Deserved love tends to leave an uneasy feeling that one is not loved for oneself; that one is loved *only* because one pleases; that one is, in the last analysis, not loved at all but used.

Cherishing

Cherishing is valuing the uniqueness of an individual. It involves sensing a child's special qualities and finding them precious. It is appreciating children for what they are, not for what they have done or what you would like them to be. When you cherish a child, you are open to the wonder of his developing self. It is a special kind of engrossment and absorption in the miracle of his existence and individuality. Apart from this awe, cherishing consists of efforts to foster the child's individuality. Implied in this is the recognition of a child's need to differentiate and separate himself from you and become an autonomous human being. If a parent prizes his own uniqueness, this separation will be much easier to accomplish.

Caring

Another pillar of love is caring, which means being interested in everything about the child — his thoughts, feelings, activities — and being concerned about what happens to him. It also means placing the welfare of the child on at least a par with your own welfare. With this kind of love, a child is inclined to think that if someone cares so much about me maybe I ought to care about myself also.

Moreover, when a child feels that a parent has his welfare at heart, he is more likely to accept the rules and regulations of the parent.

Discussion

Rather than offering "smother" love to a child ("We try to give our child everything she wants.") in which you overindulge, dominate, or overprotect the child, make your love tough in the sense that you hold your children responsible for their actions; you don't place the children at the center of your universe; and you teach them from an early age that they not only can't have everything they want but they must do certain things whether they want to or not. So parental love should be both unconditional (which provides basic security to a child) and tough (which teaches a child to be independent and responsible).

Two basic human needs are to love and be loved. Hopefully, between ages eight and-a-half to twelve, your child will begin to return your love and you will have a reciprocal relationship in which you both have the same goal: the happiness of the other person. In a mutual love relationship, the needs of the other person are as important as your own. To give is as satisfying as to receive. Of course, it takes many years before a child is able to fully leave the typical self-centered orientation and be capable of mature love. By the end of adolescence, however, your children should be exhibiting altruistic love and be able to handle close, intimate relationships with others.

ADDITIONAL READING
Fromm, Erich. *The Art of Loving.* Harper and Row, 1956.

LOVING YOUR SPOUSE

Love is strongest in pursuit; friendship in possession.

Emerson

The marriage relationship is the axis around which all other family relationships evolve. A troubled marital relationship tends to produce dysfunctional parent-child relationships. When husband and wife are primarily concerned with developing a close, loving relationship between themselves, they automatically place all other family relationships in the proper perspective.

Research has shown that the frequency of affectionate and friendly interactions between couples who have children is less than for couples with no children. The reason is that tensions and pressures increase once you are a parent and you simply do not have as much time to spend together. Obviously, if the marriage relationship is to grow once children arrive, the couple has to make a firm commitment to maintaining the primacy of their loving interactions.

Research has also shown that when husband and wife are no longer close they are more prone to fall into a maladaptive parent-child interaction pattern, such as becoming strangers to their children, relying on the children in an overdependent way, or scapegoating one or more children.

A major long-term goal of the parents, then, should be to maintain the closeness and primacy of their relationship. This doesn't just happen, both husband and wife have to work hard at keeping their relationship warm, considerate, and close. This is important because children must feel that they are not the center of their parents' world. Nor should they be the exclusive or main source of their parents' happiness. Each spouse should be the main source of pleasure for the other. Be sure your spouse knows he or she is number one on your agenda by verbal assurances and actions (be sure your spouse gets the first kiss when you get home; go out together regularly without the children; let the children know your spouse is your favorite person).

Discussion

Remember that you can't really love someone else unless you first love yourself; that is, accept and value yourself. So the bottom line in loving others is to like, be close, and be nice to yourself! There is a direct relationship between one's self-regard and the regard one feels for others. The more you work at developing yourself, the more you will be able to love others. Don't abandon or sacrifice yourself for the family.

SHOWING AFFECTION

Affection consists of expressing warm feelings of liking for a child, usually by terms of endearment, e.g., "You know, I really like you." "No matter how tired I am, I look forward to being with you." "You're my kind of person!"

Physical signs of affection include touching, hugging, kissing, and other forms of body contact. These nonverbal indices of affection tend to have a greater impact when they are coupled with direct expressions of liking and appreciation.   Thus, to show positive feelings of approval and affection, you might pat a child's head, shoulders, or hands while saying, "Good job. Well done." When you couple physical and verbal signs of affection, there is little or no chance for your child to misunderstand or overlook the fact that he or she is a likeable and valued person.

An affectionate person is direct and explicit rather than subtle about showing his love.   A subtle person shows his caring by indirect means, e.g., hard work, gifts, or self-sacrifice.   Subtle expressions tend to lack the power, punch, and directness of explicit statements.   So don't leave any doubt in your child's mind that he is liked and loved, be open and overt in expressing it.

Certain adults flinch from intimacy, avoid physical contact with a child, and find it hard to show genuine warmth.   The child is taken care of in a mechanical way and the parent remains aloof.   These parents may still go through the motions of caring, e.g., buying toys, giving spending money and the like, but they are subtly rejecting the child.   This form of emotional desertion can be more devastating than physical abandonment.   Children of cold, aloof, and indifferent parents tend to grow up either depressed and pathetic or active and disruptive, demanding to be noticed in any way, good or bad.

Guidelines

1. Expressions of positive affect must be genuine and sincere. Don't put on a show of affection out of guilt, overdependency on the child, to impress others, overpossessiveness, or the desire to manipulate the child to do something for you.

2. Ideally, children should experience affection over and over again. As a rule of thumb, you should express positive comments (affection, praise, encouragement) to a child at least three times more often than negative ones (criticism, disapproval). This holds true for adolescents as well as for younger children. Studies have indicated that the adolescent's need for affection from his parents continues throughout his teen years despite the fact that his need for control diminishes. Both adolescents and children have a need for consistent affection, i.e., don't shower them with love and kisses one moment, and then turn aloof, cold, and indifferent the next.

3. Children should feel affection from both parents. In our culture, however, men tend to find it more difficult to show affection to children. As a result, they tend to shy away from expressing their feelings and emotions which are considered unmanly. This "flight from tenderness" as it has been called, tends to lead to a closer mother-child rather than father-child relationship.

4. The *principle of reciprocal affect* states that it is a rare human being who does not respond to warmth with warmth and to hostility with hostility. Accordingly, the more you express liking for a child, the more you can expect to be liked in return. You can be pretty sure your children return your liking if the following three behaviors are present: 1) the children want you to understand them and are very open about their thoughts and feelings; 2) the children imitate your behaviors; and 3) what you think really matters to the children so that they will change their behavior to please you.

5. To assess how warm and positive you are to your children, consider the following questions: Are you absolutely crazy about each of your children? Do you smile and joke around a lot with each child? Do you frequently tell the children how much you like and love them? Do you call each child by special pet names? Do you hug, touch, and kiss your children often? Do you praise them more often than criticize them? Is your relationship with the children a "long distance" one in which there is no sharing of confidences or mutual expressions of tender warmth?

Discussion

Like praise, affection helps expand a child's self-esteem. It lifts the spirit and promotes a close parent-child relationship. It tells a child that you not only love him but like him as well. Consequently, affection increases the odds a child will identify with you and your values. Also, a child who experiences warmth and liking from his parents will be more apt to accept their discipline. In this regard it has been said that:

> *Love makes obedience lighter than liberty.*
>
> *R.W. Alger*

The challenge in giving affection is to avoid the extremes of too much and too little. In the connection, the philosopher Schopenhauer once told the following fable:*

> *One wintry day, a couple of chilled porcupines huddled together for warmth. They found that they pricked each other with their quills, moved apart and were again cold. After much experimentation, the porcupines found the distance at which they gave each other some warmth without too much sting.*

The moral of this story is that every family has to solve this dilemma – how to be close enough for emotional warmth and support, and yet not so close as to hurt each other by "smother love", overwhelming affection, and other means.

COMFORTING

> *There never was any heart truly great and generous, that was not also tender and compassionate.*
>
> *South*

Since children are relatively weak and vulnerable, they will at times become quite anxious, fearful, and distressed. At these times they

* Bellak, L. *The Porcupine Dilemma.* Citadel, N.Y. 1970.

need the reassurance and comfort of their parents. This means that you should develop the skills of cheering, calming, and sympathizing.

For example, a child who is fearful of monsters and other scary things at bedtime will be comforted just by having a parent sit by him until he falls asleep. You might also attempt to reassure him by expressing such realistic thoughts as: "There are really no such things as monsters, they are just make-believe or pretend things. Somebody like you or me thought them up. Since we thought them up, we can make them go away by thinking of something else, such as the happy times in our lives. I want you to know that your mother and I are here to protect you and make sure that no harm comes to you." Occasionally, you might want your child to take your hand while you verify that all the closets and hiding places in his room have no dangers hidden there. Of course, a child who wakes up screaming in the middle of the night because of a bad dream will need to be physically held and comforted by you.

The goal of comforting is to soothe and ease the pain of a child who is hurting — either psychologically or physically. Among the specific techniques for accomplishing this are:

1. *Cheering.* Be a model of cheerfulness and optimism. Make up for the child's pain by special care, attention, and even pampering. Express more affection. Provide the child with new toys or other objects to compensate for his pain. Do fun activities with him, such as playing games, going on trips, etc.

2. *Calming.* Be particularly calm and relaxed yourself. Be reassuring. Put the child's suffering in perspective by explaining how it is only temporary and/or that many other people have experienced similar pain. If possible, relate how you had a similar adverse experience and how you coped with it. Some parents take these opportunities to suggest to a child that pain and suffering are an unavoidable part of life and that how well one accepts it is a measure of personal courage and character.

3. *Sympathizing.* Let your child know that he is not alone in his distress, that you are concerned and share the pain with him. Be compassionate and understanding of the suffering he is going through. Do not try to down play or minimize it; rather show acceptance and respect for what he is feeling inside. Tell him you are sorry he is hurting and that his hurt is causing

you pain as well. Try to comfort or help in any way possible, e.g., holding and gentle stroking.

Children (and adults) readily display their bruises and cuts in order to reap sympathy. This craving for comforting and succorance in a time of distress seems universal. Be generous in your compassion. It is the hallmark of a loving person.

Discussion

Learn to soothe with your hands, shelter with your arms, and mollify by holding the child on your lap. Let the child symbolically return to the womb at times and be cuddled and smothered with reassuring words. This craving to let down exists in all of us — even in the man who appears strong and self-assured. We tend to feel the need for comforting the most when we are suffering from feelings of hurt, weakness, or self-doubt. So indulge your child with comfort at times and don't let the child feel this need is a sign of weakness. For instance, if your child's dog just got run over by a car, be sure to cradle the child in your arms, while expressing how sorry you are over the mishap and encouraging the child to cry it out. Let the child be emotionally dependent on you for a time until he regains composure and strength.

SHOW RESPECT

Children are usually more willing to listen to adults outside the family because they talk with them more as equals. Parents tend to talk down to or "at" children and emphasize their superiority. The more parents do this, the less children are apt to respect them or listen to their advice. Also, the less likely the children are to respect themselves which is so necessary for self-control.

Most of your interactions with children should be democratic rather than authoritarian in nature, i.e., you should treat them as people equal in worth and dignity, rather than treating them as inferiors. Avoid a master-slave relationship in the home with the children acting as slaves or servants.

Do's and Don't's for Showing Real Respect for Children

1. Don't interrupt or contradict them during a conversation.
2. Don't use verbal put downs, such as:
   "That's enough from you."
   "Get out of here!"
   "You talk too much."
   "Shut up!"
3. Do use reasoning rather than physical punishment.
4. Do ask children for advice, aid, or information.
5. Don't interfere with a child's own unique ways of being happy.
6. Do listen to children and take their opinions seriously.
7. Do show consideration for a child's feelings about things.
8. Do be courteous in both word and deed as per the following:

Courteous Actions

Respecting a child's right to privacy by knocking before entering his room; not opening his mail or private drawers; not monitoring his conversations with his peers; and not reprimanding him in front of his siblings or friends.

Courteous Words

"I'm sorry to trouble you."
"Would you be so kind as to do me a favor?"
"Won't you please?"
"Would you mind?"
"Thank you."

9. Do try to imitate a child's behavior since this is the highest form of praise. For example, you might say, "Let me see if I can do that puzzle as quickly as you did."
10. Do repeat or write down what a child has said . . . , e.g., "I like the way you said that. Let me write it down before I forget it!"
11. Do respect a child's views even when you disagree with them and convey this respect to the child.
12. Do tell your child you believe his needs are as important as yours and thus you will search for a solution which meets everybody's needs when a conflict arises.

13. Do respect yourself as much as the child and do not let the child be discourteous to you.
14. Don't joke or otherwise speak disparagingly about your children in front of them, e.g., "I wish Joan would stop eating. She's getting so fat it's repulsive."
15. Do give your child time and space to be alone, to think, work, and play in privacy.
16. Don't talk down to your child, and don't talk baby talk. Rather, let children know you are talking to them as equals.

ESTABLISH MUTUAL TRUST

To be trusted is a greater compliment than to be loved.

J. Macdonald

Trust can be defined as a firm belief in the honesty, integrity, and reliability of another person. Mutual trust between parent and child is an important aspect of their relationship because it directly influences the amount of defensiveness present in the relationship and through defensiveness, the quality of the communication. You must earn your child's trust by being generally honest and reliable. This means that you should avoid deliberately deceiving your child. Truthful answers should be given to a child's questions, even about such traditionally taboo topics as death and sex. Children's questions, such as "Where did I come from?" or "Will it hurt when I go to the doctor's?", should receive accurate responses.

In addition, parents should never make promises to a child unless they intend to keep them. Children tend to equate an adult promise with an oath. As a result, they find it difficult to trust someone who breaks a solemn pledge. So develop trust by saying what you mean and meaning what you say!

Apart from your own honesty, you should cultivate an attitude of expecting truth from your children. Once children have reached the age of reason, you should build truthfulness by tending to believe what they say (unless it is clearly false). Try to avoid saying, "Are you sure that's the truth?" or "Now, don't lie to me!" Always give a child the benefit of the doubt and he will try to live up to your trust.

False accusations from a parent who has jumped to conclusions inspired by circumstantial evidence – without waiting to hear the child's side of the story – can be devastating to a child. Until you have positive proof that the child is the offender, you must give him the benefit of the doubt. If you don't, you will have a hard time convincing the child that trust and loyalty exists between you.

When it is clear that your children have been dishonest with you, your attitude should be one of faith and confidence that they will change and overcome this weakness in the future. Once your children realize that an honest admission of wrongdoing to you always works to their advantage, you will have few instances of "cover up" behavior on their part.

In general, then, you should convey your confidence in the basic integrity of the child and indicate that you trust the child to act in accord with the respect you hold.

Discussion

One sign that children trust you is that they will come to you when they have a problem because they know you will give a straight answer. Another sign is that children feel they can confide in you and share secrets because they know you will not betray their trust.

Genuineness

Genuineness basically means to be oneself, without trying to play a role or hide behind a facade. It means an absence of phoniness, superficiality, or any kind of pretense in relating and communicating with children. By being straight-forward, you generate trust and confidence in your children.

Authenticity first of all requires that you be objectively aware of what you are thinking, feeling, and doing. If you are angry you are aware of it. If you are doing well at a task, you know it. Apart from self-awareness, being genuine means being open with the children about your thoughts and feelings. When you are not doing well you can say you are discouraged. When you are angry at a child, you can directly confront a child with your feelings rather than taking it out on the child in subtle ways. When you don't know something, you can be honest and say "I don't know." You'll be surprised how an admission of ignorance increases your credibility with children and sparks their desire to find out things for themselves.

Admit Mistakes

Being authentic also involves admitting weaknesses and mistakes. Parents invariably make a lot of mistakes in raising kids. If these errors occur within a context of a reasonable, kind, and loving relationship with children, they can be admitted and quickly corrected with no irreparable harm having been done. The kind of person you are and your relationship with the kids is more important than occasional errors. Thus, rather than having your children try to live up to an impossible image of parental infallibility, you should forthrightly admit your mistakes in dealing with children and apologize.

For example, if you yelled at your child for a minor infraction of the rules when the real reason was your tiredness, irritability, and crankiness, honestly admit the true cause to your child. You might say, for example, "Amy, I got mad and shouted at you before, but I can see now that you didn't do anything that was really that bad. I was feeling tired and out-of-sorts and I took it out on you. There's no excuse for that, I'm sorry!"

The more you quickly, frankly, and empathically admit your mistakes, without excuses, the more likely the following consequences will occur:

1. Your children will admit their own errors without excuses or deception. This honest acceptance of responsibility for one's actions will form the basis for mutual trust between you and your children.
2. Your children will view mistakes as a normal part of living and they will be more tolerant of their own shortcomings. This means they will be less likely to experience a sense of defeat from their mistakes.
3. Your children will feel reassured that perfection is not really expected of them, nor is it the price they must pay for your approval, acceptance, or love.

4. Your children will see you as more human, and thus feel closer to you.
5. The quicker you admit mistakes with absolutely no excuses, the more likely it will be that your children will forgive you and try to take your side.
6. Your children will not only trust you more but will also become less dependent on you and more self-confident.

Consistency

Apart from honesty, you establish trust by being reliable in your behaviors and how you treat a child. *Consistency* means saying something or handling a situation in the same way each time it occurs. The bedrock of a child's trust in you is the consistency with which you deal with him. When a child knows what is expected of him and how his parents will respond, he feels more secure in a world of uncertainties.

An inconsistent parent allows a certain behavior at one time and punishes it at another — often depending on mood or energy level. If a child is to hang up her clothes every day after school before she goes out to play, then her parents should check her room each day and not let her go out or talk on the phone until the task is completed. If the parents should let the child forget one day or do the job for her, then it will only take longer before this habit is firmly established.

Consistency also means that you have the same attitude towards the children day after day. In other words, you would generally not fluctuate from being loving, cheerful, and appreciative toward the children one day, and being an angry Scrooge or sad recluse the next. If you do find yourself regularly vacillating like this *for no* apparent reason, then you should seek professional counselling.

Intra-personal consistency refers to the behavior of one parent over time; inter-personal consistency refers to similar behaviors by both parents. Frequently parents do not share similar goals, expectations, or standards for children. As a result, one parent will set a limit for a child while the other tries to be a good guy and undo the discipline of the spouse. For instance, one parent will attempt to enforce an 8 P.M. bedtime rule while the other parent will try to circumvent the enforcement with such comments as "Oh, let them stay up a little longer." or "Just one more story and then they'll go to bed." Not to be outdone, the first parent subsequently begins the bedtime routine a little earlier in anticipation of the spouse's stalling maneuvers — and a vicious cycle has begun with the children caught in the middle. Parents should discuss their differences and try to work out compromises they both can live with. Of course, no one can be perfectly consistent in raising children because we are human beings, not robots. No parent would ever want to be an exact carbon copy of the other. Nevertheless, we should not give up the struggle to be generally consistent and reliable in our reactions to children, to make consistency in childrearing the *rule* rather than the *exception*.

BE A COMPANION

It is given to many to have children, but to comparatively few to know and understand them and to be companions to them.

D. A. Thom

Being a *companion* means establishing a warm, friendly relationship with your child. It is a fellowship that gradually develops from toddlership to adulthood. Initially, it will be up to you to develop the degree of companionship, but as your children mature they will play an increasing role in determining both the quantity and quality of your friendship. The basic ingredients of being a companion to a child are to spend time with the child and make sure the time spent together is mutually enjoyable.

Time Alone With a Child

There is nothing you can give your children that will make them happier or feel more important than your time and undivided attention. When you ask a child why another child is causing trouble, he will most likely respond, "He's trying to get attention." or "He just wants to be noticed." People need each other and are the greatest source of satisfaction for one another. By being with your children you will not only be helping them act and feel good, but you will be creating the opportunity for a real close relationship to develop.

Try to spend some time every day alone with each of your children. Make sure the time really belongs to the child, no interruptions, no preoccupations. It's a time when you and the child are alone together and there is a chance for mutual play, work, or intimate talk. You might want to schedule some time each day for a child so he can count on it and doesn't have to grab so much time and attention during the rest of the day. The crucial sign that you are positively involved with your child is that you enjoy the time alone together. Every child likes to feel that each day, even for just a short time, he or she is the only one you are thinking about.

To give a child time is a more meaningful gift than praise or material rewards. The gift of time requires an investment of yourself; no such investment is required in momentary praise or tangible gifts. The gift of your time and yourself is in the fullest sense the gift of your love.

A recent study* of American parents who reside in cities disclosed a very startling finding in that the average father spends only 12 minutes a work day caring for his children, and only 27 minutes on his day off. Comparable figures for working wives are 50 minutes a workday and 38 minutes on a day off. Clearly, then, the typical American city child is not being spoiled with individual attention or interaction with both his parents!

Mutually Enjoyable Times

Because so many of your interactions with children are discipline-oriented, it is important that you have other less serious interactions which are aimed at mutual enjoyment and relationship building. By playing together you help instill a feeling of companionship and closeness. Play serves many purposes, including adding adventure, excitement, and zest to life.

* *Parenting.* The Association for Childhood Education International, Washington, D. C., 1973.

Guidelines for Playing With Children

1. Schedule regular play time each day to have fun with your children. Make it a ritual that you don't forget. Also, have other special times with each child, e.g., monthly movie together, yearly trip to a state fair.
2. In playing with children, adults often interfere with the play, attempting to make the behavior more serious, work-oriented, and mature. Thus work is substituted for play. Avoid this by keeping in mind that the primary goal of play is to have fun, enjoyment, and relaxation. Don't be overly-serious or overly-controlling. If you feel awkward or have forgotten how to play, observe your children for they will quickly rekindle the spirit of childhood in you.
3. Be an active participant in the play rather than a passive observer. Be sure there is give-and-take between you and the child and mutual participation. Discover by experience the activities that you like to do that the child also likes. Remember *mutual* enjoyment is the goal. Make sure the child shows consideration for your needs, feelings, and preferences. Unless there is reciprocity in consideration and pleasure-giving, there is little basis for friendship.
4. Try to be democratic in playing with children rather than authoritarian or permissive. In lieu of orders, give a lot of suggestions and persuasive appeals, e.g., "Let's try it this way."

Discussion

The importance of spending an enjoyable time alone with each of your children is illustrated in the following quote from a professor of psychology.*

> *Many years ago, when my boy was in second or third grade, I was on a very hectic schedule lecturing on "How to be good parents and teachers." I began to notice that I was not getting the same results with my boy that I used to. I finally decided to take a day off and*

* Sheviakov, G.V. "Some Reflections on the Problem of Discipline." In *From Learning for Love to Love of Learning.* edited by R. Ekstein and R.L. Motto, Bruner/Mazel, New York, 1969.

spend it alone with the boy on the beach. We did. We played with balls and kelp and did all the things one does on the beach. At the end of the day I was completely exhausted and even my boy was kind of tired — but extremely happy. On the way home, he said quite suddenly, "Didn't we have a good time?" After I agreed, he said, "You know, I am going to do everything you ask me to do from now on."

Apart from aiding in discipline, the advantages of playing with your children include:

1. You help a child learn how to relax and enjoy life to the fullest.
2. You promote a closer relationship with the child. In this regard, studies have shown that merely being with a person while he is enjoying himself increases that person's liking for you.
3. You build a child's self-esteem. In play, children feel more assertive and self-confident. Traditional roles are reversed since children have the opportunity to teach their parents something, such as the intrinsic satisfaction and pleasure of play.
4. You can gain valuable insights into the inner thoughts and feelings of a child through the medium of play.
5. You can help develop a child's socialization skills, e.g., how to take turns, how to share, how to be empathic, how to make others happy.

ADDITIONAL READING

Sutton-Smith, B. and Sutton-Smith, S. *How to Play with Your Children (and when not to)*. Hawthorn Books, New York, 1974.

Schaefer, C., Ed. *Therapeutic Use of Child's Play*. Aronson, Publisher, New York, 1976.

CREATE AN ENJOYABLE HOME ATMOSPHERE

The less you can enjoy, the poorer and scantier yourself; the more you can enjoy, the richer and more vigorous.

Lavater

Enjoyment has to do with the quality of life in your home, which means much more than a rich material standard of living, good conduct, or high achievement levels. It has to do with valuing happy, giving, growing, creative, and warm children more than strong, moral, successful, nearly perfect, better than others, smarter than others type of children. Making your home a pleasure and joy to be in does not come easily, it takes a lot of soul-searching and hard work for most of us to create this type of environment. We have to decide such basic questions as whether we are living to work and achieve or whether we are working and achieving in order to really live and enjoy ourselves and our family. If you can answer yes to most of the following questions, the chances are good that you have the type of friendly, fun-filled home atmosphere which produces happy children.

- Do family members assign a higher priority to the enjoyment of each other and of daily living, than to achievement or "peace and quiet?"
- Can the general mood of the parents be described as happy, agreeable, and pleasant?
- Do parents often play with children where the sole object of playing is mutual fun and delight?
- Are family members friendly to one another?
- Are family trips and outings a regular occurrence?
- Do the parents make the children feel that their friends are welcome at home?
- Is one day a week set aside as family day when the whole family stays together?
- Are parties or family gatherings with relatives a regular happening?
- Are any hobbies or arts-and-crafts projects a joint venture between parent and child?

- Does the family play sports together on a regular basis?
- Are parents confident enough to act like a child at times, e.g., have pillow fights or play peek-a-boo?
- Are the parents primarily interested in seeing their children happy rather than perfect?
- Do parents and children enjoy a quiet relaxing time together each day?
- Are the facial expressions of the parents generally ones of pleasure and approval?
- Do the parents smile or laugh a lot while interacting with the children?
- Are parents and children affectionate with each other, i.e., kiss, touch each other?
- Do the parents regularly go out alone for their own enjoyment?
- Are family vacations an annual event?
- Are the parents consistently and predictably cheerful?
- Do the parents enjoy watching their children grow up — are they filled with wonder?
- Do the parents regularly bring home surprises and treats for the children?
- Do parents know how to use a light, humorous touch to relieve tension and/or motivate kids?

Discussion

One of the most important lessons you can teach your children is to take the time to relax, to do what they like, and enjoy themselves. Usually a happy child is a good child. The best way to teach, of course, is to model this attitude of not taking life so seriously all the time. If many parents were to take the time to record how they typically spend their time during the week, they would discover that almost all their time is spent taking care of chores, duties, and obligations and almost no time doing what they like. Enjoying self and family just does not seem to be as important as learning, achieving, and acquiring things.

DEVELOP FAMILY SPIRIT

Happiness in a family is unique, the product of endless labor, never ending struggle.

Time Magazine, March 28, 1977

Parental efforts directed at developing a real family orientation in their children can pay rich dividends. Children need to feel part of a larger social unit and to feel responsible for it. They need to think in terms of a we/us/our point of view rather than an I/me/mine. A close companionship family does not just happen, you have to promote it by stressing the importance of human relations within the family, of mutual acceptance, belonging, enjoyment, and consideration.

Ways of developing a sense of family include family council meetings, frequent family activities, and family projects such as designing a family coat-of-arms or family flag. Family game time for a half hour after dinner is another good custom. Each family member should have the opportunity of choosing the family game, e.g., scrabble, monopoly. Family meal times, which stress mutual sharing of experience and enjoyment are also important. In other words, you want to have a family life that has as many shared and mutually enjoyable experiences as possible.

Parents should also attempt to directly teach children values that will promote a family feeling, i.e., cooperation, friendliness, sharing, and family loyalty. For example, you might make comments such as:

"In this family, we all help one another."

"We're the Andersons, and we don't do things like that."

"We have our own way of doing things in this family."

"I'm really proud to be a member of this family."

"We may not have much money, but we all like and enjoy each other in this family."

Appeals to common values, customs, and routines can help minimize personal conflicts between parent and child. Thus, you might say, "In this family everyone is expected to make his own bed."

In brief, family spirit involves both family pride (liking, respect, and admiration for each other) and family cohesiveness (tendency to stick together). Most families will tend to come closer together in times of crisis or adversity, i.e., wars, economic misfortunes, sickness, and natural disasters. This same close family spirit can be deliberately fostered by parents during normal times. The willingness of your children to modify their personal goals when these goals conflict with the more pressing needs of the family will indicate to you the general strength of your children's commitment.

In this age of individualism, declining moral values, and a "do-your-own-thing" attitude, it seems particularly important to instill in your children a concern for the common good.

Discussion

To increase the sense of family tradition and history, Alex Haley, the author of *Roots,* recommends that the children in a family go to the oldest members and get as much oral history as possible. Many grandparents carry three or four generations of history in their heads but don't talk about it because they have been ignored. Next, Haley advises that the history of the family should be written and a copy sent to every member. Included in one's family history should be family letters and other memorabilia. Finally, Haley recommends having large family reunions. The reunion gives the sense that the family cares about itself and is proud of itself. There is the added assumption that each family member is expected to reflect this pride and, if possible, add to it. The above procedures should give a sense of heritage to a family and respect for older members.

Foster Cooperation in Children

Research has indicated that American children are disinclined to cooperate with one another spontaneously. Our environment seems to provide little stimulation or encouragement for them to learn cooperation.

It would seem advantageous, then, to provide your children with cooperative learning opportunities. In these situations, children learn how to join with others in accomplishing a common task.

For example, you might ask your children to complete a jigsaw puzzle together, or to paint a joint mural on a wall. The task you select should be intrinsically appealing to children.

To cooperate effectively, the findings show that children must learn to trust one another, establish open communication, develop a liking for one another, and learn to settle differences of opinion. In order to help your children learn these skills, be sure to praise and reward them when they act cooperatively. Signs of cooperation include sharing food and possessions with each other, talking together to share your daily experiences, exchanging information and ideas, teaching special skills to one another, working on projects together, and learning to play by the rules of the game.

Discussion

Recent research has shown that frequent experiences involving cooperative interactions with others aid the development of empathy, i.e., the ability to put oneself in the place of others and understand their perspectives. Empathy, in turn, leads to feelings of mutual liking, concern, and friendliness to others.

CONDUCTING FAMILY COUNCILS

A *family council* is a formal family meeting, usually held once a week, designed to promote an open discussion of family concerns and problems. It is a time for getting things off your chest, clearing up the inevitable misunderstandings that arise in group living, settling small disputes before they build up, and planning joint family ventures.

At a family council meeting, parents have the opportunity to ask the children's advice and opinions and show children that their ideas are listened to and respected. It is also a time to teach children the principles of group decision-making. These family meetings help everyone in the family learn to negotiate and be concerned about the welfare of the entire group. Since everyone has a voice in solving problems, they are more willing to accept the final solutions.

Guidelines

At this meeting, everyone is encouraged to express themselves freely, and everyone has a vote in the final decisions. As heads of the household, parents could retain veto powers on important issues relating to the general welfare. Some parents prefer to conduct these meetings in a completely democratic manner by letting majority rule.

Rules of order for these meetings should be spelled out in advance, e.g., No talking out of turn; No lecturing, preaching, or insulting others; If disruptive, a person has to leave the meeting; Everyone is expected to contribute to solutions, not just gripe. The problem-solving efficiency of this meeting is facilitated by appointing a chairman (typically a parent in the beginning) who sends and receives messages from all group members and coordinates the activity of the group.

Discussion

Things go more smoothly in a family where all members have a voice in decisions and are skilled in resolving conflicts. However, family councils will only be effective if a spirit of mutual trust, respect, and caring is present and all members are willing to engage in compromise or mutual give-and-take to settle differences. No one — including the parents — should try to dominate the other members. Parents must learn to be patient during these meetings, since group decision making requires considerable time for discussion as opposed to simply laying down the law.

ADDITIONAL READING

Dreikurs, R., Gould, S., and Corsini, R.J. *Family Council: The Dreikurs Technique for Putting an End to War Between Parents and Children (and Between Children and Children)*. Henry Regnery, Chicago, Illinois 1974. Complete details for setting up a family council.

INDIVIDUALIZE

We live too much in platoons; we march by sections; we do not live in our individuality enough.

E. H. Chapin

In school, a child tends to be treated as one of a group with similar characteristics. There is considerable pressure towards group conformity. But each child needs to be treated as someone unique if he or she is to develop their individuality. So observe and interact with each child on an individual basis to really get to know their needs and personalities and to help them know and value themselves. The truth is, each of us is special and unique and we need to recognize these individual differences in our children.

Fairness in raising children does not mean you treat every child exactly the same but that you do not show favoritism or special liking or love for one child. Rather than saying, "I love you both the same," say, "I love you both a lot but in different ways."

Some children just require more parental attention than others because of personal characteristics, e.g., hyperactivity, slow learning, physical handicaps. The other children in the family will understand that these children will require a little more of their parents' time.

Knowing your child as an individual is a sure sign that you care about him. One positive way to do this is to carefully watch and listen to your children to find out what they are really like. By attentive and persistent observation you will get to know their characteristic temperaments, abilities, traits, fears, hopes, and dreams — indeed, their own personal life-styles. This sensitivity to the uniqueness of children will help them become more "tuned in" to their distinctive characteristics and individuality.

Discussion

A pitfall to avoid in parenting is an unrealistic even-handedness approach to raising children. This leveling approach is evident in such reactions as treating sick children as if they were well, treating young children as if they were older, or treating neighborhood children as if they were your own. It is also seen in treating children as adults, e.g., holding up the evening meal until your husband comes home even though all the family members are extremely hungry.

The even-handedness approach takes no account of crucial individual differences in temperament, in age, in emotional maturity, or in physical strength or dexterity. Be sure to guard against responding in a stereotypic manner, i.e., responding to an adolescent rather than to a unique person who happens to be an adolescent.

Another pitfall to avoid is comparing a child with another sibling or child — either favorably or unfavorably. Thus, you should never say, "Why can't you be as studious as your brother John?" Every child wants to be treated as a unique individual and not in competition with his brothers or sisters for your love and approval.

DEVELOP POSITIVE
PERSONAL CHARACTERISTICS

Your personality and character are likely to be more influential in raising kids than any technique you might use. In other sections of this book, the importance of a number of specific personality traits were discussed, e.g., understanding, empathy, love, and genuineness. In this section, several other desirable personal characteristics will be described.

The basic assumption of this section is that you must be prepared to develop aspects of your personality to win your children's affection and to encourage them to identify with you. Children tend to find it difficult to care about personal values and ideals unless they have first learned to care about their parents. The following personal traits seem particularly conducive towards building a relationship of mutual love and liking with your child.

1. *Be Agreeable.* Be disposed to find something in a child's statement that you can agree with. Seek accord, aim to please, and be conciliatory. Show the desire to want to find areas where you and the child think alike. The more your child perceives his attitudes and values as similar to yours, the more likely he will be to identify with you and your values.

2. *Seek Self-Knowledge.* Parents should constantly be examining themselves so that they can understand their own weaknesses and problems and be on guard against projecting these onto the children. It is very easy to overvalue or undervalue children for personal reasons, or treat them as if they were persons from your past. When you have personal or marital problems, there is a tendency to take these problems out on the kids. The more well adjusted you are, the freer from distortion will be your relationships with your children. In this connection, Balzac said: "Nothing is a greater impediment to being on good terms with others than being ill at ease with yourself." Also, to effectively help children, studies have shown that it is best if children perceive you as being able to solve your problems and manage your own life.

3. *Be Patient.* Patience or the ability to delay your responding at times is needed to cope with children who can be *very* irritating. Like most personal traits, patience can be developed if you work at it. What does it mean to be patient with children? The following are some thoughts.

- Letting children learn things for themselves – often the slow or hard way.
- Letting children make many decisions themselves, even if it does take a while for them to decide what kind of treat they want.
- Allowing children considerable time to master new skills. Expect to teach them the same thing over and over again. Expect many mistakes.
- When you find yourself getting mad at the kids for some little thing they did, ask yourself, "What's wrong with me – what personal weakness of mine is causing me to lose control?"
- Recognizing that a child moves at a different pace and tempo than you.
- Listening and concentrating on what your child has to say, even though you have a million other things to do.
- Staying calm when you have to repeat directions a second and third time.
- Showing a child how to complete complex tasks, e.g., making a birdhouse, rather than just doing it yourself.

- Allowing your child to *fully* express himself without your acting bored or annoyed.
- Trying to respond to your child's needs when you are on the phone.
- Waiting and letting your unconditional offer of love and warm affection take effect.

4. *Show Cheerfulness.* Cheerfulness is closely related to humor, joy, and play; it is blocked by criticism, hostility, worry, impatience, and self-pity. According to the theory of "Psychosynthesis," it is one of the signs of a psychologically sound, fully integrated individual. Develop cheerfulness by being optimistic, i.e., looking on the bright side of things; by reflecting on the value of cheerfulness; and by developing the habit of telling yourself positive things, e.g., "Smile", "I'm going to have a good day today." You should also practice living with enthusiasm, i.e., whatever you are doing at a given moment, do it with zest and relish. Don't let parenthood become a grim, joyless, serious endeavor. Also, don't burden or depress those around you by dwelling on your minor aches and pains and small disappointments. Remember that everyone is carrying some kind of a load.

5. *Be a Positive Leader.* Rather than pushing kids all the time, try to inspire them to want to do things of their own accord because you have made things seem so attractive. Adults who have this charisma or special quality of leadership tend to be enthusiastic, optimistic, adventuresome, fun-loving, visionary, spirited, praising, and appreciative. They emphasize their love for things and the pleasure of the act, rather than linking the activity with duty or fear. They motivate by persuasive appeals and positive reinforcement rather than force.

6. *Be Sensitive to a Child's Needs.* Being sensitive means being responsive to the needs of the children. In this regard, there have been studies of the incidence of crying in infants who were either not responded to or whose crying was immediately responded to by parents. The results indicate that highly responsive mothers, the ones who were labelled "sensitive," had children who cried less than mothers who were less responsive. Other studies have found that a disposition to

obedience emerges when a child is raised in a responsive, accommodating environment. It seems that reciprocity or mutual consideration develops, i.e., the more responsive and attentive you are to children, the more responsive they will be to your needs and desires.

7. *Keep a Sense of Humor.* Humor is a rare and precious gift that only humans possess. All of our lives would be happier if we could learn to laugh at ourselves more and not take things too seriously. An often overlooked but very effective way of relieving tensions and conflicts between parents and child is humor. The quality of humor should never be lacking in dealing with children. Indeed, many situations can best be handled by a humorous or light-hearted comment from you. Humor can reduce the strain not only in yourself, but in your children. If you make somebody laugh, he cannot possibly remain angry at you. In using humor, the goal is to make your child laugh with you at the situation or at yourself, never to make light of the problem or belittle the child by ridicule, sarcasm, or mockery.

General Principles of Emotional, Social, and Moral Development in Children

General Principles of Emotional, Social, and Moral Development in Children

All parents function as child psychologists whether they know it or not. The more you know about the characteristics, thoughts, feelings, and behaviors of children at different ages, the better able you will be to understand and guide them wisely.

The purpose of this Appendix is to give the reader a broad overview of some basic concepts and principles of child development. The focus of the Appendix is on the emotional, social, and moral character development of children, rather than on cognitive or physical growth. It is felt that knowledge of child development will assist you to make more effective use of the skills and techniques presented in this book. You should also be more confident in your parenting if you know what to expect from children at different ages and levels of development. Armed with developmental information, you will be in a better position to be responsive to the needs of children at every stage of their development.

General Concepts of Child Development

The behavior of children is constantly changing and developing in lawful, regular ways. Not only is there a strong predisposition for children to develop in healthy, adaptive ways (mentally and physically), but each stage of development tends to build upon the previous one so that behavior becomes more differentiated and hierarchically integrated as a child matures. At times, children will move rapidly in an area of development, then long periods of very slow growth will prevail. Also, rather than developing in a steady, continuous straight line upwards, the growth of children tends to be spiral in nature, that is, children will move ahead a little in learning or emotional adjustment, then circle around or regress to an earlier level where they will reconcile their old and new behavior patterns, and then advance again to a higher stage of development once consolidation has occurred. Consequently, parents should expect backward moves in children's development and not become anxious or upset by them. It would be unrealistic, for example, to expect that a child would have no more "accidents" after one day's success in potty training.

There are many interrelated parts to a child's development, i.e., cognitive, physical, emotional, social, and moral. The close interrelationship of these behavioral domains is seen in the fact that retarded physical growth will impede a child's emotional and social development; also, emotional or social problems can interfere with the physical and intellectual development of children.

Developmental Stages

Although a child will follow his own individual rate of development in different areas, there seems to be definite stages or steps of growth that all children go through in the same sequence. For example, children tend to sit before they stand, to babble before they talk, to say no before yes, to draw a circle before a square, to play alone before playing with others, to be selfish before they are altruistic, and to be dependent before they are self-sufficient. All the different abilities of a child seem subject to laws of growth. Dr. Arnold Gesell of Yale University made some of the most careful observations of the growth curves of children. Knowledge of the behavior norms published by Dr. Gesell* and his colleagues should assist parents to develop realistic expectations for their children's behavior. Once you know a child's current stage of development and the next higher level, you will be in a better position to encourage the child to progress, e.g., you might provide him with challenges that are just slightly above his current level of functioning.

Children advance from one developmental stage to the next for two main reasons: maturation and environmental stimulation. Maturation means development which is a function of age or time; it refers to physiological changes in the body. No amount of practice on tasks for which a child does not have the necessary physical readiness will help him to master them. Thus, it would be foolish to try to teach 18 month old children how to read or try to toilet train 9 month old children – they simply are not developmentally ready for this. However, maturation alone will not produce the highest level of development in behavior. The child needs his parents to provide desirable growth-inducing challenges or developmental pressures. Optimal development, then, is a function of the interaction of maturation and environmental stimulation. Thus, *you must gear your childrearing practices to the child's developmental stage!*

How will you know when to exert some pressure on a child to advance to higher levels of development? You should have some general idea of what he is capable of by reading child development texts which describe the characteristics of children his age, by talking to his teachers, and by observing his friends – all this with an open mind. Your final decision must then be individualized for your child – based upon your knowledge of his unique rate of development in an area, his particular personality characteristics and cognitive abilities, etc.

Stability of Behavior

Behavioral stability means that adult behavior is predictable from childhood behavior. With respect to normal behaviors, research findings support the

* Gesell, A. and Ilg, E.L. *et al. The Child From Five to Ten.* Harper, New York, 1946.

common sense conclusion that, "As the twig is bent, so grows the tree." Once a child reaches about age 10, it seems that most normal behavior patterns tend to remain stable through adulthood. Thus, if a child shows strong achievement strivings in elementary school, he will probably continue to exhibit these strivings in adulthood.

Only when the behaviors of children are at odds with the norms of expectations of society is there a strong tendency toward change from childhood to adulthood. For example, passive-dependent behaviors tend to decline in boys as they mature, while aggressiveness has been found to diminish in girls as they develop into mature women. After reviewing the literature on child development, Professor Jerome Kagan of Harvard University concluded that children retain an enormous capacity for change when it comes to pathological behavior, and that they have a tremendous resiliency or capacity to bounce back from severe traumas or blows to their psychological security or self-esteem. These findings should be most reassuring to parents – particularly oversolicitous or overanxious parents. There seem to be few, if any, *irreversible* traumas that children can experience as a result of your childrearing.

Theories of Child Development

Most theories of child development describe an orderly, sequential process with the child developing more complex skills that build upon earlier ones. At each developmental stage there are usually one or two tasks that the child must accomplish if he is to mature. Among the major theories related to the personal-social development of children are those of Sigmund Freud, Eric Erickson, and Abraham Maslow. A brief description of each theory follows.

Freud's Theory of Psychosexual Development

According to Freud, children have a natural drive toward maturity which goes through a sequence of four stages. Arrested development at any stage can lead to psychological problems later on in life which must be "worked through" in therapy. The four major stages of development in Freud's theory are: (1) oral stage; (2) anal stage; (3) phallic stage; and (4) genital stage. Each stage is characterized by a different erogenous zone from which the primary pleasure of the stage is derived. Freud's theory focuses on a basic biological drive, i.e., to obtain pleasure – which he equated with sexuality.

The oral stage of development concerns the first year of life. The child's major need in life, feeding, is met by oral gratification (sucking, eating). The child is totally dependent on his mother at this stage for protection, comfort and security. If feeding and/or weaning problems develop during this period,

an "oral fixation" may result which means that during later stages of development the child may seek excessive oral gratifications (e.g., overeating, smoking)
to compensate for the pleasure or security he missed at this stage.   At the
second stage, the anal stage, a major task required of the child is toilet training.
The child derives pleasure during this period from elimination functions. Parental anxiety and/or undue pressure during toilet training can lead to later difficulties in elimination, such as bedwetting, soiling, constipation. On a broader level,
basic personality types can result from unmet anal needs, e.g., an "anal reten-
tive" person is described as obsessive, constricted, introverted, and a miserly
hoarder of possessions.   Freud sees the child at the anal stage as being very
egocentric, i.e., concerned with his own needs and possessions while showing
little or no concern for others. At this age parents begin to ask the child to submit
his will to others; they attempt to make demands and set limits on the child. This
leads to the negativism of the "terrible twos" which is a natural tendency of the
child to assert his growing feeling of independence and selfhood.

During the phallic stage (spanning the years from about 3 to 12), children
show an early tendency to develop Oedipal feelings.   After discovering his
genitals at about age 3, the child begins autoerotic stimulation. Too much
parental restriction at this stage can lead to impaired self-confidence and di-
minished curiosity. It can also produce anxiety about the body and its natural
functions, particularly concerning sexual functions. Self-exploration of genitals
leads to primitive sexual feelings which the young child tends to direct to the
parent of opposite sex. A natural rivalry tends to develop then between the
child and parent of the same sex for the affection of the other parent. The
child soon learns that he cannot defeat one parent for the attention of the
other so he learns to suppress his Oedipal feelings and identify with the same sex
parent.   The resolution of the Oedipal conflict signifies the beginning of the
latency period which constitutes the second part of the phallic stage. This
period lasts from about 7 years of age until puberty. The latency period is so
named because it is a time when sexual drives tend to lie dormant. The child
has many developmental tasks to master at this stage, including school achievement, peer relationships, and establishing moral or ethical principles. Upon
completion of the phallic stage, the child progresses to the final stage of development − the genital stage. Sexual interest in the opposite sex reappears when the
child enters this stage. This is the adult stage of functioning and signifies that
the child has successfully completed the process of psychosocial development.

Erickson's Eight Stages of Personality Development

Erickson was strongly influenced by Freud, but he advocated a strong social as
opposed to biological point of view in accounting for personality development.

His eight stages of development are related to the learning or developmental tasks that must be accomplished at each stage. Satisfactory learning of each task or crisis is necessary if the child is to manage the next stage satisfactorily. Erickson postulated the following eight stages of development:

1. *Learning Trust vs. Mistrust.* If made to feel loved and secure by his parents during the first year of life, the infant develops trust in adults, a sense of security, and a basic optimism. A child tends to develop trust in his relationship with his parents if they respond promptly to his cries, keep him warm, dry, and well-fed, and provide him with considerable amounts of physical holding and cuddling. From this basic trust comes a sense of security and self-acceptance.

2. *Learning Autonomy vs. Shame.* Between about 18 months and 3½ years, the child is faced with the task of learning control of both his impulses and elimination functions. Perhaps the biggest task of this stage is toilet training and parents are advised not to start this process until the child is physiologically ready (between 15 to 30 months) and to avoid shaming or punishing the child during the training. If handled well, the child will emerge from this "law and order" phase with a sense of independence and autonomy, with pride in his self-controls. The oppositional tendencies of this age help him develop a feeling of being independent from his parents and feed his new-found awareness of self as a separate entity.

3. *Learning Initiative vs. Guilt.* During the period of about 3½ to 6 years, children are exploring everything as a means of finding out more. They not only physically intrude into cupboards and drawers, but they verbally intrude into other people's interactions, demanding attention. Children also spend considerable time in dramatic make-believe play during this period. Play is a very serious business during childhood and through it a child learns to try out different roles, to imagine the consequences of different courses of actions, to relate to other people. If well-handled a child will not be made to feel guilty about fantasy-play or inquisitiveness, and will take the initiative in relating to others and exploring the environment rather than hanging back in a fearful way.

4. *Learning Industriousness vs. Inferiority.* During the grade school years, a major task of children is to learn to be industrious, to develop good work habits, and to complete tasks. They learn to respect the rules of a game and to develop self-confidence in their abilities, to do well in work and play — both in school and at home. They do their chores at home conscientiously and reliably. They also perceive that they are successful at making friends. It is very important that children this age experience some area of success where it is clear that they are achieving and pleasing their parents and other adults as well as themselves. Even if a child's

ability and interest lie in activities not valued by parents, they should make a special effort to encourage and support any areas of competence.

5. *Learning Identity vs. Identity Diffusion.* During the adolescent years, the child is engaged in the major task of resolving the question, who am I? He will experiment with different roles, consider different occupations, seek more and more freedom and responsibility at home, reject certain values and develop others — all in the effort to establish who he is and what he wants out of life. It is very helpful for adolescents to be members of a family where the parents are committed to basic beliefs and values, but where the children are given freedom to choose their own values and life styles.

During adulthood and old age, Erickson theorizes that a person goes through the last three stages of development: learning intimacy vs. isolation; learning generativity vs. self-absorption; learning integrity vs. despair. During the later part of adolescence or in young adulthood, achieving true intimacy in a relationship with another person is a major focus, while becoming successful in your job and as a parent is the challenge during early adulthood. If all the other stages of development proceed normally, one reaches the final accomplishment, integrity of your personality which leads to inner peace and happiness.

Maslow's Hierarchy of Needs

Like Freud and Erickson, Maslow conceptualized a hierarchical growth of the human personality. Concentrating on human needs, Maslow stated that there are some basic needs that must be satisfied before one can even think about developing his higher level needs. At level one Maslow places the physical needs of man, i.e., hunger, freedom from pain. Level two is associated with the basic needs for safety and security — both physical and psychological. Only when one feels confident that he can count on food, clothing and shelter, as well as the unconditional love of his parents, does one tend to reach out to others to develop close interpersonal relations, i.e., reach level three which represents the social needs of caring and interacting with others. Level four concerns the development of achievement needs by accomplishments in school and at work. At the highest level Maslow postulates the need for self-actualization, i.e., the complete realization of one's abilities and interests. Examples of fully actualized persons, according to Maslow, are highly creative, productive people who are free to do their own thing and who love what they are doing. After studying these people extensively, Maslow concluded that they tend to be vigorous, full of zest for living, humorous, imaginative, and open to mystical, transcendental experiences.

One common assumption of all three theories of development described above is that a child can move on to the next more advanced stage of personality development only after he has successfully completed the requirements or tasks of the previous level. This insight can provide parents invaluable understanding into the personality development of their children.

Developmental Tasks for Parents

The aforementioned theories described, from differing perspectives, the basic needs and developmental tasks that are common to children as well as the general patterns of development that are characteristic of most children at certain ages. Parents also face certain tasks at each stage of a child's development.

Infancy

Being responsive to the infant's needs is perhaps the major task for parents, e.g., paying prompt attention when the baby cries. You *can't* spoil an infant with too much attention, rather it gives security to infants to have their basic needs responded to with few frustrations. The sense of self of the infant is too immature to cope with many frustrations and delays. By being responsive to a baby's needs for food, warmth, physical comfort, sleep, and cuddling you develop basic trust in the child towards you.

Another task for parents is adjusting to the inevitable stresses of living with a new baby. During infancy a child is totally dependent upon his parents for survival. Infants make continual demands on their parents for time and attention. The disruption a firstborn infant creates in the household is hard to imagine — the infant just home from the hospital cries an average of an hour and three quarters a day. A colicky baby seems to be continually upset — both day and night. As a result, fathers often feel jealous of the attention mothers must give to infants. Many fathers tend to find fault with their wives during this period, which only compounds the tensions within the home. Hard work, sacrifice, and sharing responsibilities are the order of the day with infants around. They test the strength of your marital relationship as well as your personal adjustment.

The Preschool Years

By the second year of life, the child is no longer a helpless, completely dependent infant but begins getting into things and behaving in ways at odds with parental wishes. So now parents attempt to change children's behavior against their wills while the kids attempt to have their way despite knowing what the parents want. So a conflict of wills emerges and the parent's role makes a dramatic shift from primarily being an affectionate caretaker to being a disciplinarian or teacher. The feelings of affection and trust generated during the caretaker period will undoubtedly affect a child's receptivity to parent discipline at this stage.

The major task of parents of preschoolers, then, is to gradually socialize the child by setting limits. They must help a child learn controls by being firm but loving. Rather than acting like dictators and expecting instant obedience, parents should allow for delay and grumbling when a direction is given. Be firm but realistic. Children must learn early that there are two very different kinds of activities for them: those things they must do whether they like it or not, and those things they can do or not do as they like. This takes time so begin early and don't expect self-control to develop all at once or once and for all.

Rather than saying no to everything a preschooler does parents should use distraction a lot. Young children thrive on variety and change of pace. Thus, when you see children getting bored or restless, head them off at the pass by providing new activities which will interest them.

Another task of parents is to encourage play and fantasy behavior while simultaneously providing the child with reality testing experiences. So help children discriminate between real and pretend objects and events without inhibiting their fantasy life or enjoyment of play.

The Grade School Years

Children this age must be doing things, they would rather not sit for long periods of time. During the elementary school years an important task for parents is to provide constructive outlets for the abundant energy of children and to ensure some success experiences. The school age child acquires self-esteem from what he or she can do, from being competent at school work, sports, and making friends. They are introduced to the world of work through chores at home, homework, and classroom assignments. Their work must be supervised to ensure that they learn correct work habits and attitudes. Also, parents should encourage children to develop special interests and skills by providing them with the necessary materials and instruction.

Although parents are still the primary source of support and influence for school age children, their world of social influence is widening. Another task for parents, then, is to learn to be part-time parents, that is, share their child with teachers and peers.

The Teenage Years

The parents of adolescents face the primary task of giving their children the necessary freedom and autonomy to find out who they are as persons. They must learn to think for themselves, develop their own values, and make their own decisions. By giving ever increasing areas of freedom and responsibility you gradually turn over to them control over their lives. Adolescents should have few areas of decision-making that are not their own. Your role as parent now is to be consultant rather than disciplinarian in that you give more guidance rather than external controls.

While granting independence you must still be available to offer affection, understanding, and advice. This is no easy task since teenagers not only show open rebellion, animosity, and criticism towards parents, but they are difficult to talk to at this age. Teenagers just don't want to listen anymore to parents since they see it as a way of being controlled and kept dependent. While letting go of your adolescents, you still must give them the feeling that you are on their side, that you have faith in them, and are pulling for them. The teenager is trying to go in two directions at the same time, namely, be independent yet stay somewhat dependent upon you. The more you encourage the independent striving by treating them as adults, the more they will act like grown-ups.

The adolescent is fundamentally insecure, which is expressed by restlesssness, addiction to fads, and resistance to authority. They face a number of serious challenges and important decisions, including vocational choice, heterosexual adjustment, formation of a philosophy of life, and development of basic values. Parents must give adolescents the understanding, respect, and confidence they need to face these important challenges. Parents should also allow them to rebel in relatively insignificant areas, e.g., manners or dress, rather than in areas of greater importance, e.g., behavior which is inconsiderate or harmful to others.

Children's Emotional Development

At birth the emotional reaction of infants is not well differentiated. New babies show a generalized excitement which encompasses situations of discomfort, fear and anger. As they grow older, infants' emotional expressions become more clearly distinguishable so that a 10 month-old baby will exhibit identifiable signs of fear, anger, and satisfaction. With further maturation, the child's inner drives and impulses come into inevitable clashes with the demands of reality outside the self. Not only is conflict an unavoidable part of growth, but so is insecurity and anxiety. Being relatively weak and vulnerable during most of their youth, the children naturally feel some tense and uncertain moments in coping with the new challenges that they are continually experiencing.

It seems that the golden years of childhood contain more conflict, aggression, anxiety, and lonliness than most of us can recall.

Aggression

Through the first two years of life the child is self-centered and has a low frustration tolerance. Seeking to have their own way, these children tend to resolve conflicts by becoming overly aggressive, i.e., hitting, grabbing, biting. Consequently, social conflicts among preschool children are usually frequent and characteristically violent. Fortunately, aggression tends to be short-lived at this age so that preschoolers will be locked in intense combat one minute and playing happily the next.

Much of human aggression can be traced to frustration; it is just impossible to rear children without frustrating many of their desires or wants. As children grow up they learn more adaptive responses to frustration than directly acting out their angry feelings. Parents must encourage more adaptive reactions by indicating to a preschool child that they will not tolerate aggressive solutions to problems. Among the alternate responses that you can teach a child are the following: to verbally express disapproval; to develop a future time perspective; to be empathic to the needs and feelings of others; and to negotiate conflict by a give-and-take procedure. Throughout grade school, children show increasing control of their emotions so that there are less and less frequent temper outbursts. Crying as a mode of expression also decreases.

Childhood Fears

Fears can be described as responses to immediate and evident danger. They are distinguishable from anxiety which is an apprehensive response to possible threat. What a child fears has been found to differ with age and experience. From the relatively few, simple fears of the infant (fear of sudden movements, falling, and loud noises, fear of strangers), the fears of children become more numerous, abstract, and complex with age. During the preschool years, fears of animals, the dark, physical hurt, and imaginary creatures (ghosts and monsters) increase.

The preschool period is a naturally fearful period of development and parents should not become unduly alarmed when a child wakes up screaming after a nightmare. Most of these fears will pass with age. Remember not to deny the existence of the fear ("There's nothing to be afraid of."); rather, be accepting, understanding, and help the child verbally express the fear and thus gain greater control over it. You might suggest ways of coping with the fear such as imagining oneself yelling and hitting the imaginary creatures until they run away. You can help prevent fears in young children by keeping your own fears under cover and avoiding the use of fear-inducing threats such as "The boogey man will get you if you don't behave."

At the elementary school period, fears of animals, monsters, and the dark decrease but fears relating to school — including worry about grades and fear of teachers — increase from ages 9 to about 12. In general, the fears of grade school children diminish in both number and intensity as they learn to cope with new situations and overcome feared events. However, they still harbor a great many more fears than parents commonly realize. Studies show that about 80 percent of the children this age are afraid of dying or being killed, as well as being afraid that someone in the family will become ill or have an accident. About 70 percent of the children this age express the fear that their house might burn down, or that they might be kidnapped. Since so many children express these numerous fears, there is no reason to assume that they are unduly anxious or emotionally disturbed. Only when a child's fears seriously interfere with his functioning, i.e., doing things that other children do, should a parent become concerned.

Although many childhood fears decline and seem to disappear, a fairly large number of these fears persist in one form or another into adulthood. One study revealed that over 40 percent of childhood fears continued strong into adult life, e.g., fear of snakes and certain animals, fear of bodily harm by fire, illness, or drowning; and fear of threat associated with the supernatural (the dark and being left alone).

A recent survey of 500 high school students revealed that they remain fundamentally insecure and list the following 15 situations as the most threatening to them, listed in descending order:

1. Being teased or laughed at (boys felt most threatened when their masculine image was threatened; girls, when their desirability or popularity was questioned).
2. Death of a parent.
3. Facial or bodily injury.
4. Divorce of parents.
5. Terrible arguments with parents.
6. Being harshly criticized in public.
7. People who seem insane.
8. Arriving at a party where there are mostly unfamiliar faces.
9. Being caught in a lie publicly.
10. Moving to a brand new community.
11. Violent or "bullying" peers.
12. Failing an exam.
13. Terrible arguments with friends.

14.   Being rejected by a member of the opposite sex.

15.   Becoming addicted to alcohol or drugs.

So adolescence is a time of dilemmas (being independent yet still wanting the security of parental dependency) and important decisions; insecurity and anxiety seem to be the rule, as opposed to the intense fears of early childhood.

Children's Social Development

During the preschool years, children's interactions with their peers show clear age trends: solitary play, parallel play, and cooperative play. For the first two years children tend to play largely by themselves, even when others are close by. From about three to five, children will copy the behavior of their peers. If peers are riding tricycles, a child will ride his tricycle also. By age three the child can engage in cooperative, give-and-take play with peers, not just parallel play. They can wait, share, and take turns, and accept substitute toys. However, they are still egocentric and show little consideration of other children's feelings. They have little empathy or capacity to put themselves in another person's position and take that person's point of view. It is this immaturity, not perversity, which makes a preschooler continue to pester her mother after she has been told that mommy has a headache and wishes to be left alone.

In grade school, the loosely knit play groups of the five-to-eight year olds develop into gangs or cliques. A gang is characterized by its longevity, solidarity, and group loyalty. A clique is a smaller, more informal, intimate social group. It exists not to compete with other groups but for the mutual satisfaction and good times of its members. The grade school child likes peers of the same age and sex. About ages eight and a half to ten, the "chum" or special friend period arrives. Intimacy with a chum sets the stage for later heterosexual intimacy in adolescence and adulthood. If there are frequent family moves during this period which interfere with the development of close friends, then later social development may be retarded or impaired.

Friendship means a sincere liking between two people. By age three or four a child is usually able to identify a "best friend." These early childhood friendships are less intense than adolescent friendships, but they nevertheless are important in that they overcome loneliness, self-centeredness, and boredom. They also offer support and encouragement, teach a child to solve conflicts by compromise, provide feedback about self, and encourage the sharing of personal experiences. For the school age child, the best friend or chum is usually the one who lives nearby, can play with him, share things, have fun together, and engage in the same kind of activities. The adolescent, on the other hand, seeks a more intimate kind of friendship, that is, the sharing of secrets and confidences, trust and loyalty, and the opportunity to talk and talk and not get bored.

It is evident that the friendship experiences during each of these three stages of development prepare the child for the next higher form of friendship.

Self-Esteem

A generally accepted theory relating to the development of self-esteem in children is that a child's self-regard is profoundly influenced by the significant adults in his life, especially his parents. The noted psychiatrist Harry Stack Sullivan maintained that a child's sense of self is developed by the process of "reflected appraisals." In other words, as significant persons appraise him so in time will the child come to value himself. Praise, approval, and acceptance by parents, then, seem especially important for young children since these reactions generate the beginning of positive self-regard in the child. If you are constantly saying no and disapproving of the child's behavior, then it seems likely that he will soon disapprove not only of his actions, but of himself as well.

Maladjustment in Children

There is no precise, sharp differentiation between normal and abnormal behavior. Most, if not all, pathological behavior in children has a normal counterpart at an earlier age level. Diagnosing maladjustment or emotional disturbance in children requires an intensive, professional study of the child, including his motives, temperament, typical social interactions and current stresses and pressures. A variety of surveys have indicated that about 10 percent of school age children in this country have emotional problems, although only about 1 percent of the child population receives professional assistance. One reason is parental resistance to seeking outside help for psychological problems although parents regularly bring their children in for physical checkups.

How can you tell if your child is experiencing an emotional difficulty that warrants outside help? Some indicators are that his or her deviant behavior has persisted beyond the expected age; the behavior is frequently displayed and easily aroused; and ordinary educational efforts to change the deviant behavior have failed. Other criteria of abnormality are the extent it interferes with the relationships between the child and other people — both adults and peers; the extent it may handicap a child at a later date (e.g., a learning disability); the degree and duration of regression or return to an earlier level of development that is present; and how much inner turmoil or loss of self-esteem it causes the child.

Development of Moral Character

Morality can be defined as the direct internalization of external cultural norms. According to cognitive-developmental theorists, there are universal ethical principles which are distinguishable from arbitrary conventional rules and beliefs. These theorists further assume that moral development — like intellectual and personality development — follows an invariant developmental sequence that is influenced by maturational and environmental factors.

Kohlberg's Developmental Theory

After extensively studying the development of moral judgment across different cultures, the psychologist Lawrence Kohlberg concluded that character development progresses hierarchically through three general levels. At the first stage, called "Preconventional", the preschool child responds to parental labels of good and bad but interprets these labels in terms of either the physical or pleasurable consequences of actions (punishment, rewards) or in terms of an elementary notion of reciprocity, e.g., "I'll scratch your back if you scratch mine." At the second or "Conventional" level, the grade school child perceives that following the regulations of parents and society is valuable in its own right, regardless of the immediate and obvious consequences of an act. The child's inclination is not only to conform to conventional norms of morality but to be loyal to and actually maintain, support, and justify these norms. The child tends to identify with the person or group involved in giving the orders or setting laws. At this stage, the child begins to experience some guilt after a transgression, rather than just fear of punishment. When asked why a behavior is wrong a child at this stage will say because it "isn't nice or good" or it's "against the law." At the highest level, called "Autonomous" or "Principles," there is a clear effort for adolescents and adults to define for themselves moral principles (equity, justice) that have validity apart from the authority of persons or groups holding these principles.

Kohlberg has found that the great majority of Americans reason about moral issues at the conventional level.

Piaget's Developmental Theory

A number of years before Kohlberg's formulation, Piaget also postulated three general levels of moral development. The first stage, termed the "Morality of Constraint", lasts until the child is seven or eight years old. It is characterized by blind obedience to parents, with adults regarded as omnipotent. The child views punishment in terms of such primitive concepts as "imminent justice" and "moral realism." The former refers to the idea that all bad acts will be punished by either human means or by natural or supernatural forces. The latter pertains to a child's evaluation of actions in terms of consequences rather than in terms of intentions or motives.

Between the ages eight and ten, the child goes through an intermediary stage
of adherence to rules in which he either internalizes the rules without judging
them, or alternates in his responses to situations. At the final level of moral
development, rules merge into abstract principles around the age of twelve,
and the child begins to evaluate intentions and circumstances rather than deeds
or outcomes alone. Moral principles such as love, justice, and honesty come to
form the basis for morality rather than rigid rules or fear of punishment. Moreover, cooperation and mutual respect among peers takes the place of the former
unilateral respect for adults.

Summary

Both Piaget and Kohlberg describe a developmental thrust in the child to move
from initially acting appropriately out of fear of punishment; to conformity
out of respect for law and authority; to moral behavior based upon an inner
conviction and belief in basic ethical principles. To help a child advance to the
next higher level of moral development, parents should not only model the more
mature moral behavior, but also discuss with the child the need for law and
order and the rationales underlying such universal ethical principles as the
Golden Rule, and Equality Among Men. Even more importantly, parents should
realize that respect is the primary root of morality — respect for oneself, for
others, for authority; if you are continually berating or belittling authority
figures (police, mayor, president of the nation, teachers, bosses), how can you
expect your child to respect them?

Studies have shown that by age ten, in most cases, the moral character of
the child is likely set for life. A further finding is that to a startling degree,
each child learns to feel and act, psychologically and morally, as just the kind
of person his or her parents have been in their relationship with the child.
So the early parent-child interactions seem to form a child's character to a
substantial degree. It makes a difference if your interactions with a child
are accepting vs. rejecting; approving vs. disapproving; affectionate vs. cold;
responsive vs. indifferent; empathic vs. misunderstanding; respectful vs. dis-
respectful; kind vs. cruel; and enjoyable vs. grim.

The golden rule is the most universally accepted expression of good character.
So teach a child to love, i.e., an attitude towards people which includes un-
selfishness, consideration and understanding of others, cooperativeness, kindness,
and altruism. The child learns best to love by being loved; to be just by receiving
just treatment from parents. The first decade of life is the most important one
for moral development. The continuous daily experiences with parents determine a child's character in large measure. These experiences teach the child
right from wrong and the value of self and others. Good character is based on

love of self and others, then, and the joy of giving rather than fear of punishment. Good moral character cannot simply be taught in the schools; it must be
learned and lived in the home. In this sense, the prime responsibility for its
development rests not with teachers or friends, but with parents.

INDEX

INDEX